HASSAN FAKI

With the Compliments of
MUSLIM WORLD LEAGUE
LONDON OFFICE

To...

AIMS AND OBJECTIVES
OF ISLAMIC EDUCATION

AIMS AND OBJECTIVES
OF ISLAMIC EDUCATION

edited by

Syed Muhammad al-Naquib al-Attas

HODDER AND STOUGHTON

KING ABDULAZIZ UNIVERSITY, JEDDAH

British Library Cataloguing in Publication Data

World Conference on Muslim Education,
 1st, Mecca, 1977
 Aims and objectives of Islamic education.
 – (Islamic education series).
 1. Islam – Education – Congresses
 2. Education – Aims and objectives – Congresses
 I. Title II. Al-Naquib al-Attas, Syed
 Muhammed III. King Abdulaziz University
 370.11   LC904

ISBN 0–340–23607–8

First printed 1979
Copyright © 1979 King Abdulaziz University, Jeddah

Phototypeset in V.I.P. Baskerville by Western Printing Services
Ltd, Bristol. Printed in Great Britain for Hodder and Stoughton
Educational, a division of Hodder and Stoughton Ltd., Mill
Road, Dunton Green, Sevenoaks, Kent by Hazell Watson &
Viney Ltd, Aylesbury, Bucks.

Foreword

بسم الله الرحمن الرحيم

For the first time in 1977 Muslim Scholars from different parts of the world met at the First World Conference on Muslim education organized by King Abdulaziz University, Jeddah, Mecca and held at Mecca from March 31 to April 8 and tried to study and analyze basic problems, state the aims and objectives of education and recommend the methods of implementing them. This is the first attempt of its kind to remove the dichotomy of religious and secular education systems that are at present operative in Muslim countries. The scholars did not want this to be achieved by a superficial mixture of secularized and religion-oriented courses. That was why they had to restate the nature of man, the purpose and goal of his existence and the central role of education in helping man to achieve this end. Fourteen committees deliberated on fourteen different topics.

In the general recommendations of the entire Conference board definitions of concepts and attitudes were made. As these are at the root of the scholars approach to religion and education we quote below this whole section:

'The aim of Muslim education is the creation of the "good and righteous man" who worships Allah in the true sense of the term, builds up the structure of his earthly life according to the Sharia (Islamic law) and employs it to subserve his faith.

'The meaning of worship in Islam is both extensive and comprehensive; it is not restricted to the physical performance of religious rituals only but embrace all aspects of activity: faith, thought, feeling, and work, and in conformity with what Allah (praise be to Him) says the Holy Quran, "I have created the Jinn and man only to worship Me" and "say, O My Lord; my prayers, my sacrifice, my life and my death are for Allah, the Lord of the Worlds Who hath no peer."

'Therefore, the foundation of civilization on this earth, the exploitation of the wealth, resources and energies that Allah has hidden in its bowels, the search for sustenance, the measures by which man can rise to full recognition of the ways of Allah in the Universe, knowledge of the properties of matter, and the ways in which they can be utilized in the service of faith and in the dissemination of the essence of Islam and in helping man to attain to a righteous and prosperous life – all these are considered forms of worship by which scholars and God-seekers come into closer contact with Allah. If such is the Islamic concept of worship and from the Islamic point of view the object of education in the most comprehensive sense of worship is the upbringing of the true believer, it follows that education must achieve two things. First, it must enable man to understand his Lord so that he worships Him in full conviction of His Oneness, observes the rituals, and abides by the Shariah and the Divine injunctions. Secondly, it must enable him to understand the ways of Allah in the universe, explore the earth, and use all that Allah has created to protect faith and reinforce His religion in the light of what Allah has said in the Quran.'

'It is He who hath brought you from the earth and made you inhabit and inherit it'.

Thus the sciences of the Sharia meet other sciences such as medicine, engineering, mathematics, psychology, sociology, etc. in that they are all Islamic sciences so long as they move within the framework of Islam and are in harmony with Islamic concepts and attitudes. All these sciences are necessary in reasonable degree for the ordinary Muslims, while at the same time they are in a much more specialized form, required and sought by scholars, *Mujtahidun* and Jurists of the *Ummah* (the nation).

'The Islamic concept of science does not impose any restriction or limitation, empirical or applied sciences except for one limitation which pertains to the ultimate ends on the one hand and their actual effects on the other. In the Islamic sense science is a form of worship by which man is brought into closer contact with Allah; hence it should not be abused to corrupt faith and morals and to bring forth harm, corruption, injustice and aggression.

'Consequently any science which is in conflict with faith and which does not serve its ends and requirements is in itself corrupt, and stands condemned and rejected and has no place in God's injunctions.

'Every system of education embodies a particular philosophy which emanates from a particular concept, from which it cannot be isolated. We cannot have a philosophy or an educational policy which is based on a concept not identical with the Islamic. This is what is now happening when we apply British, French, American or Russian with reference to the 'liberal' concept of man, and values that humanists believe in (which even a modern unchristian or anti-religious thinker like Bertrand Russell used to stress), is wanting in relevance. This conclusion has been reached by secularist-modernists only because they conceive education as a process that helps man to live well in this material world. They do not believe in fundamental, unique, immutable, moral or spiritual values.

The humanists also deny the concept of man that 'revealed' knowledge has given to us. They conceive education as a continuous process of mental, emotional and moral development, as initiation into a quality of life which helps man to see different points of view and the relationship of these various points of view to one another. As Professor Peters says, 'The great teacher is he who can convey this sense of quality to another, so that it haunts his every endeavour and makes him sweat and yearn to fix what he thinks and feels in a fitting form. For life has no one purpose, man imprints purposes upon it. It presents few tidy problems; mainly predicaments that have to be endured or enjoyed. It is education that provides that touch of eternity under the aspect of which endurance can pass into dignified, wry acceptance, and animal enjoyment into a quality of living'. (*Education as Initiation*, University of London, 1964, p. 48).

The unfortunate thing about this attitude is its vagueness. It considers education as having 'no ends beyond itself'. It makes a person as Newman rightly pointed out, 'a gentleman' and not necessarily a 'religious man'. The spiritual world or the world after death does not have any relevance to the process of cultivating this quality. 'Humanistic thinking', as another humanist has said, 'is the cultivation of man, his self-cultivation and self-unfolding into full humanity'. (Laszo Versenyl: *Socratic Humanism*, New Haven, 1963). What this cultivation of self means to a modern humanist has been explained by Hitt in his book entitled *Education as a Human Enterprise* (Washington, 1973). It means the cultivation of a scientific attitude which means rejection of dogma, questioning absolutes and, instead of faith, reliance on reason alone. It stresses human values and the complementary roles of science and human values.

It is this concept of man which humanists preach that differs fundamentally from the concept of man that religion gives us. In so far as values are concerned there appears to be a good deal of similarity. Both humanists and religious thinkers agree on the 'objective' status of values but humanists think that through man's efforts the value concept has emerged and man's rationality has succeeded in formulating an objective concept of man. But there is a possibility of further improvement, modification and change. The religious thinker, on the other hand, says, 'It stands to reason, that, if education is supremely concerned with the quality of people, it needs the inspiration of some vision of what human beings ought to be – some notion of what is a good kind of person. This is a moral and spiritual quality and one to which it is very difficult to get a clear and united answer in these days of confused and disintegrating values.' (*Aims of Education*, M. V. C. Jeffreys, 1972, p. xiv). The humanist approach is ineffective in such crucial days as these only because if man is the sole arbiter of his own destiny and vision, if man is imprinting his own purpose on life, there is no reason why man cannot change it and imprint upon life a completely new purpose and thus discard the old purpose. The very disintegration of values can be justified from this point of view. If there is nothing absolute, constant change and fluctuation of aims and purposes is the logical outcome. It is obvious that humanists get defeated by secularist-modernists and then start asserting only the rational element in man or, like Bertrand Russell, fall back on certain values which are considered genuinely 'human'. Religion, on the other hand, places man in a very large perspective – the perspective of eternity and infinity. Man partakes of that eternity and infinity through his spirit which alone is regarded as the custodian of eternal Truth. This philosophy has a long-standing tradition and it has proved its worth by creating those devotees whose character and action have earned the approval of man all the world over and in all ages.

Religion thus provides an all-comprehensive norm of man and an all-inclusive goal for education. This norm has a stability because the values are regarded as absolutes derived from the absolute attributes of God which are being continually realized in a relative context in time and space. Contextual change only leads to change in emphasis and focus, modification and alteration of stress and relative importance of certain values in different periods and areas. It does not mean any change in values. Religion thus provides a meaningful goal for education. According to religion this goal is revealed to man and thus it has an objective status. It is not concocted by man or just derived from experience. All experience is tied down to time and space, hence relative. But this goal is verified by experience as the most desirable one because it has succeeded in transforming barbarous people like the pre-Islamic Arabs into the most advanced, civilized and cultured people of the world and produced individuals of unquestioned character and sterling merit.

Islam has made this goal the most balanced and comprehensive conceivable in the world. Man is regarded as potentially the vicegerent of God on Earth. God has given man authority over entire creation. In order to realize this authority in actual life man must acquire wisdom which transforms him into a good man and at the same time turns him into a wise master. Education is that process which helps man in acquiring this wisdom. It is therefore a comprehensive process because it trains emotional, intellectual and sensual faculties simultaneously. God has revealed to man his nature and the laws that lead man to the total efflorescence of his personality. Man is expected to learn through experiments and work out the details of that process whose broad foundations are given to man in the Quran and whose human example is historically preserved in the life, activities and sayings of Prophet Muhammad, peace and blessings of Allah be on him.

One great advantage that this concept has over the humanistic concept is that it provides a supreme ideal and an unshakable norm for educationists to aim at when they are planning the education system and working out the methodology. It saves man from drifting. It has also a remarkable advantage over a similar concept of Man given in other religions because Islam presents a universal and rationally acceptable norm. It provides the concept of one God, one humanity and one religion from the days of Adam. As such the norm of human values is considered to be the same for all humanity in all ages. Moreover it saves man from being proud and teaches man humility by creating in him the feeling that all power of man over Nature or himself is power delegated to him by God. It is not his own. This concept leads man to a better understanding of others and to peace and happiness among nations and races.

Last but not least, the total framework of values is also dependent on the concept of faith in the hereafter. Man is to consider this life not as an end in itself but as a process that is leading to a complete and better life in the hereafter. Thus the attitude that is cultivated is one of acceptance of faith and action according to a norm. In order that action may lead to the betterment of man and society, a methodology of self-analysis and criticism and social criticism is taught which generates acutely sensitive individuals fully aware of rights, duties and responsibilities and thoroughly conscious of their own shortcomings. As love of God and the Prophet are the major means of acquiring this sensitivity, this methodology includes both intellectual awareness and innate response. Moreover as the whole of creation is regarded as potentially controlled by and for man, science and values are made to play complementary roles with values providing guidance and aims. This is far more satisfying than the dry intellectualism of humanism because it gives cardinal importance to love and hence to human sensibilities.

In this book writers have tried to analyze these principles in some detail. As this is the first time that scholars have tried to restate the Muslim approach in the context of modern life and the invasion of Muslim education by the secularist-modernist approach and ideas, these writings may be regarded as an attempt to explore the problem, state the Muslim approach and indicate how the aims and objectives of education can be made truly Islamic. That is why Professor Naquib al-Attas has critically examined the Western secularist approach and stated an Islamic model of higher education, Professor Qutb has analyzed the conflict between the modernist and Islamic approaches to various branches of knowledge, M. A. K. Brohi has stated the broad comprehensive approach of the Muslims which supersedes narrow distinctions, and Dr. Hadi Sharifi has reinforced the conclusions of these writers by a comparative analysis of Western-secularist and Islamic philosophies of education. Dr. Moazzam Hussain on the other hand gives the historical evolution of the Muslim classification of knowledge and systematization, and Dr. Zaki Badawi sees how modern scientific knowledge and the Islamic tradition can be complementary and not contradictory. Dr. Abdul Haq Ansari indicates the necessity of a new perspective and Prince Muhammad shows us how the Quran can be a source of new strength in this context. These essays initiate the discussion which, we hope, will lead to positive research and consolidated formulations.

We have added a bibliography, which is not intended to be complete, but which is a select bibliography of important writings on the Islamic philosophy of education.

King Abdulaziz University,   Syed Ali Ashraf
Jeddah   General Editor

Contents

Appendices

Introduction

The aim of education in Islam is to produce a good man.[1] What is meant by *good* in our concept of 'good man'? The fundamental element inherent in the concept of education in Islam is the inculcation of *adab* (*ta'dib*),[2] for it is *adab* in the all-inclusive sense I mean, as encompassing the spiritual and material life of a man that instils the quality of goodness that is sought after. *Education* is what the Prophet, Peace be upon him, meant by *adab* when he said:

ادّبني ربّي فأحسن تأديبي

'My Lord, educated (*addaba*) me and made my education (*ta'dib*) most excellent.'

There is a general tendency among Muslims who are aware of the dilemma that is now pressing upon the Community to see its causes as *external*, as coming from the outside, originating from influences exerted by Western culture and civilization. That its causes are attributed to external elements is of course based upon correct observation, but it is also only partly true. It is true that the Muslim mind is now undergoing profound infiltration of cultural and intellectual elements alien to Islam; but to say that the causes are derived from external sources is only *partly* true. How has it been possible in the first place for Muslims to succumb to such infiltration to the extent that their predicament has now assumed the proportions of a dilemma? We will at once realize that the external causes referred to are not the only ones responsible for throwing us into a state of general crisis, and we must see that the full truth of our answer to the question lies undeniably in the prevalence of a certain anomaly within our Community; an anomaly that has with increasing persistence plagued our world and our intellectual history, and that has been left uncorrected and unchecked, now to spread like a raging contagion in our midst. Only by our consciousness and recognition and acknowledgement that serious *internal* causes have in fact contributed considerably to our general disarray will we be able to discern the full truth that lies at the core of the dilemma we suffer today.

1

We can never resolve this dilemma unless we know why we have allowed ourselves to be so weakened as to be susceptible of straying away from the right path. One of the definitions of knowledge is to know the cause of the existence of a thing, for knowledge of the cause or causes is itself a partial solution to the problem. And this brief discussion on external and internal causes is meant to create the awareness that the internal causes are prior to the external and as such the former have primacy over the latter, so that their clarification demands our urgent attention. This introduction will attempt to clarify the problem.

As to the internal causes of the dilemma in which we find ourselves, the basic problems can – it seems to me – be reduced to a single evident crisis which I would simply call the *loss of adab*. I am here referring to the loss of *discipline* – the discipline of body, mind, and soul, the discipline that assures the recognition and acknowledgement of one's proper place in relation to one's self, society and Community; the recognition and acknowledgement of one's proper place in relation to one's physical, intellectual, and spiritual capacities and potentials; the recognition and acknowledgement of the fact that knowledge and being are ordered hierarchically. Since *adab* refers to *recognition* and *acknowledgement* of the right and proper place, station, and condition in life and to self-discipline in positive and willing participation in enacting one's role in accordance with that recognition and acknowledgement, its occurrence in one and in society as a whole reflects the condition of justice. Loss of *adab* implies loss of justice, which in turn betrays confusion in knowledge. In respect of the society and community, the confusion in knowledge of Islam and the Islamic world-view creates the condition which enables false leaders to emerge and to thrive, causing the condition of injustice. They perpetuate this condition since it ensures the continued emergence of leaders like them to replace them after they are gone, perpetuating their domination over the affairs of the Community. Thus to put it briefly in their proper order, our present general dilemma is caused by:

1. Confusion and error in knowledge, creating the condition for:
2. The loss of *adab* within the Community. The condition arising out of (1) and (2) is:
3. The rise of leaders who are not qualified for valid leadership of the Muslim community, who do not possess the high moral, intellectual and spiritual standards required for Islamic leadership, who

2

perpetuate the condition in (1) above and ensure the continued control of the affairs of the Community by leaders like them who dominate in all fields.

All the above roots of our general dilemma are interdependent and operate in a vicious circle. But the chief cause is confusion and error in knowledge, and in order to break this vicious circle and remedy this grave problem, we must first come to grips with the problem of loss of *adab*, since no true knowledge can be instilled without the precondition of *adab* in the one who seeks it and to whom it is imparted. Thus, for sublime example, God Himself commands that the Holy Quran, the Fountain of all true knowledge, cannot even be touched in approach save through the prescribed *adab* or ritual purity.[3] Knowledge must be approached reverently and in humility, and it cannot be possessed simply as if it were there available to everyone irrespective of intention and purpose and capacity. Where knowledge of Islam and the Islamic world-view is concerned, it is based on *authority*. Since Islam is already established in perfection from the very beginning, requiring no further developmental change nor evolution towards perfection, we say again that adequate knowledge about Islam is always possible for all Muslims. There can be no relativism in the historical interpretation of Islam, so that knowledge about it is either right or wrong, or true or false, where wrong and false means contradiction with the already established and clear truth, and right and true means conformity with it. Confusion about such truth means simply ignorance of it, and this is due not to any inherent vagueness or ambiguity on the part of that truth. The interpretation and clarification of knowledge about Islam and the Islamic world-view is accomplished by authority, and *legitimate* authority recognizes and acknowledges a hierarchy of authorities culminating in the Holy Prophet, upon whom be Peace. It is incumbent upon us to have proper attitude towards legitimate authority, and that is reverence, love, respect, humility and intelligent trust in the veracity of the knowledge interpreted and clarified by such authority. Reverence, love, respect, humility and intelligent trust can be realized in one only when one recognizes and acknowledges the fact that there is a hierarchy in the human order and in authority within that hierarchy in the matter of *intelligence*, *spiritual knowledge* and *virtue*. In respect of the human order in society, we do not in the least mean by 'hierarchy' that semblance of it wherein oppression and exploitation and domination are legitimized as if they were an established principle ordained by God. *Any* kind of

3

'hierarchy' and 'order' is not necessarily legitimate, for such order is not order at all – it is *dis*order; and *adab* is not resignation to disorder, as that would be contrary to justice. Disorder is the manifestation of the occurrence of injustice. The fact that hierarchical disorders have prevailed in human society does not mean that hierarchy in the human order is not valid, for there is, in point of fact, legitimate hierarchy in the order of creation, and this is the Divine Order pervading all Creation and manifesting the occurrence of justice. God is the Just, and He fashions and deploys all Creation in justice. In order that mankind generally might recognize and acknowledge the just order, He has bestowed upon His Prophets, Messengers and men of piety and spiritual discernment, the wisdom and knowledge of it so that they in turn might convey it to mankind who ought to conform with it as individuals and as a society. And this conformity with that order is the occurrence of *adab*; the resulting condition of that conformity is justice.

The chief characteristic symptom of loss of *adab* within the Community is the process of *levelling* that is cultivated from time to time in the Muslim mind and practised in his society. By 'levelling' I mean the levelling of everyone, in mind and attitude, to the same level as the leveller. This mental and attitudinal process, which impinges upon action, is perpetrated through the encouragement of false leaders who wish to demolish legitimate authority and valid hierachy so that they and their like might thrive, and who demonstrate by example by levelling the great to the level of less great, and then to that of the still less great. This *Jahili* streak of individualism, of immanent arrogance and obstinacy and the tendency to challenge and belittle legitimate authority seems to have perpetrated itself – albeit only among *'ulama* of less authoritative worth – in all periods of Muslim history. When Muslims become confused in their knowledge of Islam and its world-view, these *'ulama* tend to spread among them and influence their thinking and infiltrate into positions of religious leadership; then their leadership in all spheres of life tends to exhibit this dangerous streak and to encourage its practice among Muslims as if it were in conformity with the teachings of Islam. They who encourage this attitude pretend that what is encouraged is no other than the egalitarian principle of Islam, whereas in fact it is far from it in that what they propagate leads to the destruction, or at least the undermining, of legitimate authority and hierarchy in the human order – it is the levelling of all to *their* level; it is injustice.

No doubt it is possible to concede that the critics of the great and learned were in the past at least themselves great and learned in their own way, but it is a mistake to put them together on the same level – the more so to place the lesser above the greater in rank, as happens in the estimation of our age of greater confusion. In our own times those who know cannot fail to notice that critics of the great and learned and virtuous among Muslims, critics who include groups of both modernist and traditionist 'reformers', and a third group consisting of secular scholars and intellectuals, who all emulate the example of their teachers in the habit of censuring their own true leaders, are men invariably of much less authoritative worth than the lesser of the past; men whose intellectual and spiritual perception of Islam and its world-view cannot even be compared with any of those of their teachers – let alone with those of the great they disparage, from whom their teachers derived knowledge and guidance without due acknowledgement. They and their followers thrive where there is confusion and ignorance, where they can escape the relentless scrutiny and censure of knowledge. It is because Muslims in our age have become confused, ignorant and desperate that they see in them men who have, as if for the first time, opened their minds to Islam; they do not see that these men are poor imitations of the great of the past. They do not bring anything new that the illustrious Muslims of the past have not already brought; nor do they clarify Islam better to the clouded vision than the immensely superior clarification accomplished by the masters of the past. Yet, it is such as they who have been most vociferous and vehement in disparaging and denouncing the past, its great and learned scholars, thinkers and jurists and men of spiritual discernment. Their conception of the past has been influenced by Western ideas on human evolution and historical development and secular science. Although they were cautious in attempting to islamize the ideas they brought in, their ideas posed a great danger to the Muslim's loyalty to Islam because they were not ideas that could be truly islamized. They opened the doors to secularism without knowing it, for it did not take long for their followers to develop their ideas to secular proportions. Because they were never really intellectually and spiritually profound, they preoccupied themselves instead with sociology and politics, and aspects of jurisprudence that bear upon these subjects. Their experience of the decline of Muslim rule and the disintegration of Muslim empires made them take notice of Ibn Khaldun and they concentrated their efforts on the concept of *Ummah* and of the state in Islam. They naturally neglected to lay as much stress on the concept of the individual and the role the individual plays in realizing and establishing the *Ummah* and the Islamic state. Now it is true that the *Ummah* and the Islamic state are paramount in Islam, but so is the individual Muslim, for how can the *Ummah* and the Islamic state be developed and established if individually Muslims have become confused and ignorant about Islam and its world-view and are no longer *good* Muslims? When they say that the decline of the Muslims was caused by corrupt leadership, their identification of *cause* with corrupt leadership is not quite correct. If we ask ourselves what it is that is corrupt about their leadership, we will recognize at once that it is their *knowledge* that is corrupt, which renders their leadership corrupt. Corrupt leadership is the *effect*, and not the cause; and it is the effect of confusion and error in the knowledge of Islam and its world-view. If we accept this, then it ought to be clear that the root of the problem is no longer to be seen as grounded in the *Ummah* and the state. The identification of cause with the corruption of *knowledge* as here suggested, and not with that of *leadership* as they suggest, significantly shifts the ground wherein lies the root of the problem to that of knowledge, and knowledge is inherent in *man* as an *individual*, and not in society and state and *Ummah*. So, *as a matter of correct strategy* in our times and under the present circumstances, it is important to stress the individual in seeking a just solution to our problem rather than society and the state. Stressing the individual implies – as a precondition that our ideas should be equipped sufficiently to enable us to grasp and present a solution to the problem – knowledge about intelligence, virtue, and the spirit, and about ultimate destiny and purpose; for intelligence, virtue, and the spirit are elements inherent in the individual, and such knowledge is to be gained not from Western notions of psychology which are irrelevant to us, but from Islamic tradition expounded and interpreted by our masters of the past, the men of spiritual discernment. Only in this way can we conceptualize and then realize an educational system within the Quranic framework and based upon Islamic foundations that would educate generations of Muslims to come to become *good* Muslims; Muslims no longer confused, but knowing and practising, and ready to realize and establish the Islamic state and to enact their proper role as a single, vigorous *Ummah*. The stressing of society and the state opens the door to secularism and secular ideology and secular education. Now, we already possess an abundant store of knowledge about intelligence, virtue and the spirit, and of teachers in the masters of the past who were men possessed of intellectual and spiritual discernment and virtue; all

6

these – the knowledge and the men – of a universal quality and character, so that what they brought forth is valid for man for all time, since the Sources whence such knowledge comes, and the deep draughts such men drew, are of a universal nature so unique in transcending history and the forces of change, that they are always new, always 'modern'. But such knowledge and such men were precisely the ones they ignored, in spite of the fact that the Sources referred to are the Holy Quran and the Sunnah. Instead, they disparaged such men and looked for faults and condemned the men because of their faults, notwithstanding that their merits were greater than their faults. *Adab* consists in the discernment of the merits, not of the faults; for the merits determine their place in the hierarchical order.

All the three groups mentioned are prone to levelling everyone to the same level of equality, notwithstanding the fact that even in God's Sight we are not all the same and equal. Indeed, we are all the same in that we are creatures of God, human beings, cast in flesh and blood. But our spirits, our souls, though derived from that One Spirit, and though *essentially* the same are, in point of *power* and *magnitude*, not the same, not equal. We are like so many candles of varying lengths and shapes and hues and sizes; the tallow they are made from is essentially the same and the light they burn is essentially the same, but the greatness of the flame, the light each sheds, is not the same in power and magnitude. And we judge the value of the candle by the light it sheds just as we judge a man by those qualities by which he is not the *same*, but *excels* another, such as by his intelligence, virtue, and spiritual discernment. So it is neither correct nor true to regard such a man as merely a man of flesh and blood *like any other*, for he is not like any other in that his intelligence, virtue, and spiritual discernment transcend the limitations of his flesh and blood, and his greatness of spirit manifests his excellence over others. *Adab* is the recognition and acknowledgement of such lights in man; and acknowledgement entails an attitude expressing true reverence, love, respect, humility – it entails knowing one's proper place in relation to him who sheds such light.

Today we hear it often stressed that the Holy Prophet, upon whom be Peace, is no more than a man like any other man. They among the three groups referred to who propagate this may say that in our age of aberrations and excesses in belief and faith, an age in which they think that Muslims are on the verge of unbelief, it is proper and timely to emphasize the human and mortal nature of the Holy Prophet, upon whom be Peace. We answer that even if what they allege and think is true, and even if there is genuine good intention in what they do, they still fail to see that the general confusion of the Muslims has not been and is not caused by any confusion on the part of the Muslims as to the nature, personality and mission of the Holy Prophet, upon whom be Peace. Confusion in belief and faith among the Muslims has nothing to do with and does not revolve around any issue relating to the Holy Prophet's humanity and created nature. The cause lies not in confusion about the created nature of the Holy Prophet, but in *ignorance* of *tawhid* and the fundamental articles of faith and other related essentials of belief which are all comprised in that category of knowledge which we have designated as *fardu 'ayn*; and this means that the cause is part of the general cause which we have here called confusion and error in knowledge. The basic problem, therefore, is that of *education* – the lack of proper and adequate Islamic education – for such education, rightly systematized, would assuredly prevent the occurrence of general confusion leading to aberrations and excesses in belief and in practice. The rise of false leaders in all spheres of life, which follows from loss of *adab* and confusion and error in knowledge respectively, means in this particular case the rise of false *'ulama* who restrict knowledge (*al-'ilm*) to the domain of jurisprudence (*fiqh*). They are not worthy followers of the *mujtahidun*: the great Imams who through their individual efforts of sublime research established the Schools of Law and Jurisprudence in Islam. They are not men of keen intelligence and profound insight, nor are they men of integrity in keeping the trust of right spiritual leadership. Notwithstanding the fact that the Holy Quran repeatedly condemns it, they delight in endless controversy, disputations and polemics which succeed only in making mountains out of jurisprudential molehills in whose blind paths the generality of Muslims is left guideless and bewildered. Their misguidance leads to an emphasis on *differences* between the various *madhahib* and to obstinate adherence to trivialities within them, which in turn gradually incite the modernist and traditionist 'reformers' and their followers to attack falsely the *mujtahidun*, thereby undermining legitimate authority, and to discredit the concept and validity of the *madhhab* in Islamic life. The false *'ulama* are not able to develop the interpretations of the *mujtahidun* along their proper courses within clear guidelines, and their incessant elaboration of trivialities leads to neglect of the real problem of education. They are content in leaving the Muslim's basic education in *fardu 'ayn* knowledge at the infantile level while they allow the development of *fardu kifayah* knowledge to increase tremendously. In this way the amount of secular knowledge increases and develops in a Muslim's life out of proportion to the religious, so that the Muslim spends most of his adult life knowing more about the world and less about religion. Thus we have weak Muslims and weak dangerous leaders whose comprehension and knowledge of Islam is stunted at the level of immaturity; and because of this Islam itself is erroneously made to appear as if 'undeveloped' or 'misdeveloped' or left to 'stagnate'. The increase in *fardu kifayah* knowledge, and preoccupation in emphasizing its role in life without due emphasis on its acquisition being organized in proportionate balance with that of the *fardu 'ayn* at all levels of education, naturally directs the attention solely to the problems of state and society, for the state and society are the true referents in respect of *fardu kifayah*. The preoccupation in our age with the Islamic state and the *Ummah* is succinct indication of the preponderant estimation accorded to the acquisition of *fardu kifayah* knowledge. In this respect, too, the social, political, and legal sciences in that category of knowledge has been demanding – and receiving – undue attention and ascendancy over the other category in our estimation and our consciousness. It is easy to see why, under these circumstances, the trend of affairs in Muslim life leads to the 'socialization' of Islam; and the levelling of the Holy Prophet, upon whom be Peace, to the same level as the masses, is but a logical consequence of that 'socialization'. Together with 'socialization', rationalism – the kind understood in the West, that is as derived from the concept *ratio*, not the kind we mean as derived from the Quranic *'aql* – is advocated by the 'modernists' who emulate the example of their predecessors at the turn of the century. By ineptly treating the nature of revelation as if it were a natural phenomenon, and the Holy Quran as if it were created and on the same level as other books; by presumptuously 'despiritualizing' the life and person of the Holy Prophet, upon whom be Peace, they prepare the ground for a 'secularized' Islam. They draw inspiration about ideas on state, society and man not so much from Islam and Islamic sources as from Western European sources about liberty, equality, and fraternity; about the social contract and the doctrine of human rights and humanistic individualism. The successes of socialism in the West in recent times have blindly encouraged their thinking in identifying socialism with Islam – at least as a political theory and social order – as if the choice of life-style open to Muslims lies solely between capitalism and socialism!

The secular scholars and intellectuals among the Muslims derive their inspiration mainly from the West. Ideologically they belong to the

9

same line of descent as the modernist 'reformers' and their followers; and some of them cleave to the views of the traditionist 'reformers' and their followers. The majority of them do not possess the intellectual, spiritual, and linguistic prerequisites of Islamic knowledge and epistemology so that they are severed from the cognitive and methodological approaches to the original sources of Islam and Islamic learning. In this way their knowledge of Islam is at the barest minimal level. Because they occupy a strategic position in the midst of the community and unless they drastically change their ways of thinking and believing, they pose a grave danger to the Islamic welfare of the Community. They have no *adab*, for they do not recognize and acknowledge the legitimate authorities in the true hierarchical order, and they demonstrate by example and teach and advocate confusion and error. Their chief error is the levelling of the basic categories of knowledge in Islam, that is, the *fardu 'ayn* and the *fardu kifayah*, so that there is now confusion as to which is which, in that the nature of *fardu 'ayn* knowledge and its method of approach is confused with that of the *fardu kifayah*. In this way they emulate the ways of thinking and believing of Western man, and advocate such ways to their students in all spheres of life. Now, the West does not recognize and acknowledge *fardu 'ayn* knowledge as it does not even possess or know of any other category of knowledge except that which we have designated as *fardu kifayah*. This is in fact the main reason why, as demonstrated in the course of Western intellectual history throughout the ages and the rise of secular philosophy and science in Western civilization, the Western conception of knowledge based upon its experience and consciousness must invariably lead to secularization. There can be no doubt, therefore, that if the secular Muslim scholars and intellectuals allow themselves, or are allowed to confuse the Muslim youth in knowledge, the deIslamization of the Muslim mind will continue to take effect with greater persistence and intensity, and will follow the same kind of secularizing course in future generations. Large numbers among them do not fully understand the nature of Western culture and civilization whence they draw their inspiration and before which they stand agape in reverential awe and servile humility portraying the attitude of the inferior. They do not even completely grasp the contents and implications of the teachings of their alien masters, being content only to repeat them in vulgarized versions and so cheat the Muslim audience of their true worth. In deIslamizing the Muslims, and in situations where Western colonialism or domination have held sway, the Western administrators and colonial theor-

10

ists have first severed the pedagogical connection between the Holy Quran and the local language by establishing a system of secular education where race and traditional culture are emphasized. At the higher levels, linguistics and anthropology are introduced as the methodological tools for the study of language and culture, and Western values and models and orientalist scholarship and philology for the study of literature and history. Then, still being brought to bear upon the study of language and literature (which are the identifying and consolidating cultural elements of Islamization) and of history and traditional culture, sociology and educational theory and psychology are significantly introduced. These, misplaced at the purely rational disposal of scholars and intellectuals inadequately equipped with knowledge of Islam and its world-view, tend to reduce Islam to the level of other religions as if it were the proper 'subject' of the philosophy and the sociology of religion, and as if it were an evolved and developed expression of primitive religion. And all these and other fields of knowledge in the human sciences, including those philosophical elements in the theoretical aspects of the natural physical and biological sciences, instilled into the marginal minds of secular Muslim scholars and intellectuals, are such that their knowledge so conceived is productive not only of potential and theoretical confusion, but also of actual and practical error as well. Through the unbalanced assimilation and imparting of such knowledge without any islamizing science and judgement being brought to bear upon its every proposition, and the active participation in its formulation and dissemination by secular scholars and intellectuals, the rapid propagation of loss of *adab* is assured and indeed becomes a widespread reality. These false leaders among Muslims are responsible for causing the romanization of the originally Arabic script of the language and thus facilitating gradual severance from its formal, lexical and conceptual connections with the Sources of Islam, with their own Islamic sources and with the languages of the other Muslim peoples; for causing the deArabization, Westernization and confusion of the language and its semantic and general vocabulary so that many important concepts pertaining to Islam and the Islamic world-view have lost their transparency and have become opaque; for causing the emergence of the journal and the newspaper – so significantly un-Islamic in concept and purpose – and of mediocre journalists and writers of rustic quality who all contribute to the mutilation of the standards of literary values and expression established by Islam; for causing the widespread emergence of the

11

marginal Muslim and the marginal society stranger to the *Ummah*, and hence for causing the disintegration of consciousness in the ummatic solidarity; for causing the severence of the Muslim past from the consciousness of the present; for causing the establishment in our midst of an educational system designed, from the lowest to the highest levels, to perpetuate secular ideology; for causing the rise of various forms of chauvinism and socialism; for reviving the *Jahili* spirit of advocating a return to pre-Islamic values – and cultural tradition – and many more which for obvious reasons it is not necessary to detail here. And the same is true, in varying degrees of the absence of *adab* in respect of their character traits, their lack of quality, their contagious contribution to error and confusion in knowledge of Islam and its world view, and their propagation of false knowledge, of other such scholars and intellectuals among the Muslims, wherever they may be in the Muslim world, whether in the Arabic speaking regions or not. They have all become conscious or unconscious agents of Western culture and civilization, and in this capacity they represent what we have earlier identified as the *external* sources and causes of our dilemma. But their existence amongst us as part of the Community creates for us the situation whereby what was once regarded as 'external' has now moved in methodically and systematically to become internal. In their present condition, they pose as the external menace which has become a grave internal problem, for intellectually, as it were, the *dar al-harb* has advanced into the *dar al-islam*; they have become the enemy within, and – unlike the kinds known to the Muslims of the past – they are not hidden nor any longer lurking underground, but have surfaced in multitudes into the full light of awareness, advertising themselves openly and conspicuously and exhibiting their learned confusion and arrogant individualism so publicly that it is no longer possible to ignore them. The epistemological weapons they use to bring about the de-Islamization of the Muslim mind are invariably the same, and these are – apart from the underlying principles of secular philosophy and science that produced and nurtured them – anthropology, sociology, linguistics, psychology and the principles and methods of education. If the underlying principles and methods of these sciences are not made subject to some kind of Islamizing formula whereby they are rendered harmless, then, as they are, they would continue to be harmful to the Islamic welfare of the Community.

Loss of *adab*, then, not only implies loss of knowledge; it means also loss of the capacity and ability to recognize and acknowledge true leaders. If

12

all are brought down to the level of the masses, the *awamm*, how can true leaders stand out above the rest? If true leaders are denied their rightful place above those they lead, how can they be recognised and acknowledged by the led? And true leaders must not be confused with the false, for how can nightingales, put in the same cage as crows, sing? To put true leaders in lofty stations in our estimation and to put ourselves below them and to revere, to love, to respect, to affirm their veracity and confirm in our actions their wise counsels and learned teachings in humility is not to *worship* them, as the narrow-minded among the modernist and traditionist 'reformers' erroneously think. Were the Angels worshipping Adam, upon whom be Peace, when they prostrated themselves before him? Indeed, they were obeying God, Glorious and Exalted, and recognizing and acknowledging the superior knowledge bestowed upon the first men by his Creator – they not only saw the clay he is made from, but they recognized and acknowledged even more so the spirit that God breathed into him. It was Iblis who saw only the clay and refused to recognize and acknowledge Adam's superior nature, and disdained to prostrate before him in spite of the Divine Command. Recognition and acknowledgement of excellence in another does not mean regarding the other as a *rabb* and assuming an attitude of the *'abd* towards that other; it is none other than recognizing and acknowledging God's Knowledge and Will and Power and Just Purpose, His Bounty, Charity and Love in bestowing excellence in one over the other, so that that one may share it with others. But only those others who recognize and acknowledge derive benefit from it, not those who do not.

We must see that the three main groups that perpetuate loss of *adab* in our times, and that not only perpetuate, but also consolidate its paralyzing influence and intensify its odious spread among the generations of contemporary Muslims, are not in reality our true leaders. Without knowing any of them, and without being in any way guided by them, we can still know about Islam and its world view from the great *'ulama* of the past who are the real interpreters of the sources of such knowledge. Conversely, without knowing the true teachers of the past and without being guided by them, it is almost impossible to arrive at the correct understanding and knowledge of Islam and its world view. It is as if the false leaders of our times have been fashioned in the mould of the crafty Master Magician in the guise of new lamps meant to be traded for the old. They indeed claim to be the new lamps; and we must not fall into the error of the ignorant wife of Aladdin, trading the old for the new, unaware of the priceless value and wonderful quality of the old far surpassing all of the new put together. The thinking, methods and example adopted by these false leaders and their followers, (compounded of a mixture of truth and falsehood and right and wrong which are the ingredients of confusion, propagated and advocated at a time when Muslims are already confused and desperate and in no balanced state of mind and spirit to absorb more confusion), have effected among the generality who are influenced by them, a warped understanding of Islam and a clouded vision of its interpretation of the world and of reality and truth. The effect of their teachings among this generality of Muslims, particularly the younger generation who are experiencing the effects of Westernization, is the tendency towards a relentless and erroneous attitude of levelling by which they judge all things. Their words and actions betray their mental and attitudinal condition of levelling in which they imply and even understand the Holy Quran to be on the same level as other books; Islam to be on the same level as other religions; the Holy Prophet, upon whom be Peace, to be on the same level as other Prophets, Peace be upon them all, who are all regarded as being on the same level as ordinary men; *the* knowledge to be on the same level as other sciences; true leaders to be on the same level as false ones, and the greater to be on the same level as the lesser; the life of the world to be on the same level of importance as that of the hereafter. It is this levelling of everything instilled into the understanding of the masses, without due consideration being given to the quality of that understanding, and without due elaboration as to the distinctions that naturally exist in the hierarchical order of creation, especially in the human order, that is productive of the 'socialization' of Islam. The despiritualization of man, starting from the Holy Prophet himself – the despiritualization that must necessarily take place as a precondition to the levelling process – tends to involve Islam absurdly in a kind of secularization. These groups of false leaders, who are not even sure what they are supposed to do, and are equally groping for solutions to the general problems we encounter today – solutions hastily conceived in piecemeal fashion, of tentative validity and dubious soundness – have indeed misrepresented the achievements of the truly great *'ulama* of the past: the *mujtahidun*, the men of piety and virtue and of intellectual and spiritual excellence, in connection with their interpretation of Islam and its world view. Inclined as they are to see only small matters and not great ones in their estimation of superiors, they have not understood those men completely and have misrepresented them in

14

caricature before us. Our task ahead is to represent the true leaders of the past in truer light, to exercise justice in our estimation of them from whom our predecessors derived guidance and knowledge. We must reexamine the misrepresentations, referring every detail to the original sources they allegedly claim to represent; we must scrutinize their premises, their deductions and conclusions, and retrace the paths of their logic to see how far they have been correct or have been led astray by their own process of inadequate thinking; we must ourselves know the originals and understand them in their correct perspectives. It is our duty to study diligently the thoughts of the true leaders of the past, who were all recognized and acknowledged by a grateful Community; who all served Islam and the Muslims with signal merit, recognized and acknowledged by a knowing Community of contemporaries without their true characters and qualities having to be fabricated and 'built up' long after they were gone, as so often happens in our age of falsehood and confusion. We must learn from the great of the past their knowledge and wisdom. This does not mean that we ourselves cannot contribute any further knowledge that can be contributed, but it does mean that we must first draw our strength and inspiration from their wisdom and knowledge, and that when we do begin to contribute ours, we must recognize and acknowledge them as our teachers, and not disparage and denounce, for *ijtihad* can be exercised without having to undermine legitimate authority. They are like torches that light the way along difficult paths; when we have such torches to light our way, of what use are mere candles?

Syed Muhammad al-Naquib al-Attas

*Religion, Knowledge
and
Education*

Chapter One

Preliminary Thoughts on the Nature of Knowledge and the Definition and Aims of Education

Syed Muhammad al-Naquib al-Attas

Syed Muhammad al-Naquib al-Attas, Professor of Malay Language and Literature and Director since 1970 of the Institute of Malay Language, Literature and Culture, of which he was the Founder, at the National University of Malaysia, Kuala Lumpur, was born in 1931. He received his M.A. from McGill University, Canada and Ph.D, from the School of Oriental and African Studies, London. He was Dean of the Faculty of Arts at the University of Malaya, Kuala Lumpur (1968–70), Dean, Faculty of Arts, The National University of Malaysia, Kuala Lumpur (1970–73) and member of many important international associations. From 1960 to 1963 he was a Fellow of the Canada Council. In 1975 in recognition of his contribution to comparative philosophy, he was made a Fellow of the Imperial Iranian Academy of Philosophy. He has more than 14 books to his credit including such works as: *The Mysticism of Hamzah Fansuri*; *Raniri and the Wujudiyyah of 17th century Acheh*; *Sufism as understood and practised among the Malays*; *The Origin of the Malay Sha'ir*; *Concluding Postscript to the origin of the Malay Sha'ir*; *Islam in the History and Culture of the Malays*; *Comments on the Re-examination of al-Raniri's Hujjatul-Siddiq: a refutation*; *Islam: the concept of religion and the foundation of ethics and morality*.

Introduction

Many challenges have arisen in the midst of man's confusion throughout the ages, but none perhaps more serious and destructive to man than today's challenge posed by Western civilization. I venture to maintain that the greatest challenge that has surreptitiously arisen in our age is the challenge of knowledge, indeed, not as against ignorance; but as knowledge as conceived and disseminated throughout the world by Western civilization; knowledge whose nature has become problematic because it has lost its true purpose due to being unjustly conceived, and has thus brought about chaos in man's life instead of, and rather than, peace and justice; knowledge which pretends to be real but which is productive of confusion and scepticism, which has ele-

19

vated doubt and conjecture to the 'scientific' rank in methodology and which regards doubt as an eminently valid epistemological tool in the pursuit of truth; knowledge which has, for the first time in history, brought chaos to the Three Kingdoms of Nature; the animal, vegetable and mineral. It seems to me important to emphasize that knowledge is not neutral, and can indeed be infused with a nature and content which masquerades as knowledge. Yet it is in fact, taken as a whole, not true knowledge, but its interpretation through the prism, as it were, the world-view, the intellectual vision and psychological perception of the civilization that now plays the key role in its formulation and dissemi- nation. What is formulated and disseminated is knowledge infused with the character and personality of that civilization – knowledge presented and conveyed as knowledge in that guise so subtly fused together with the real so that others take it unawares *in toto* to be the real knowledge *per se*. What is the character and personality, the essence and spirit of Western civilization that has so transformed both itself and the world, bringing all who accept its interpretation of knowledge to a state of chaos leading to the brink of disaster? By 'Western civilization' I mean the civilization that has evolved out of the historical fusion of cultures, philosophies, values and aspirations of ancient Greece and Rome; their amalgamation with Judaism and Christianity, and their further development and formation by the Latin, Germanic, Celtic and Nordic peoples. From ancient Greece is derived the philosophical and epistlemological elements and the foundations of education and ethics and aesthetics; from Rome the elements of law and statecraft and government; from Judaism and Christianity the elements of religious faith; and from the Latin, Germanic, Celtic and Nordic peoples their independent and national spirit and traditional values, and the development and advancement of the natural and physical sciences and technology which they, together with the Slavic peoples, have pushed to such pinnacles of power. Islam too has made very significant contributions to Western civilization in the sphere of knowledge and in the inculcation of the rational and scientific spirit, but the knowledge and the rational and scientific spirit have been recast and remoulded to fit the crucible of Western culture so that they have become fused and amalgamated with all the other elements that form the character and personality of Western civilization. But the fusion and amalgamation thus evolved produced a characteristic dualism in the world-view and values of Western culture and civilization; a dualism that cannot be resolved into a harmonious unity, for it is formed of conflicting ideas,

20

values, cultures, beliefs, philosophies, dogmas, doctrines and theologies altogether reflecting an all-pervasive dualistic vision of reality and truth locked in despairing combat. Dualism abides in all aspects of Western life and philosophy: the speculative, the social, the political, the cultural – just as it pervades with equal inexorableness the Western religion.

It formulates its vision of truth and reality not upon revealed knowledge and religious belief, but rather upon cultural tradition reinforced by strictly philosophical premises based upon speculations pertaining mainly to secular life centered upon man as physical entity and rational animal, setting great store upon man's rational capacity alone to unravel the mysteries of his total environment and involvement in existence, and to conceive out of the results of speculations based upon such premises his evolutionary ethical and moral values to guide and order his life accordingly. There can be no certainty in philosophical speculations in the sense of religious certainty based on revealed knowledge understood and experienced in Islam; and because of this the knowledge and values that project the world-view and direct the life of such a civilization are subject to constant review and change.

The inquiring spirit of Western culture and civilization originated with disenchantment towards religion as that civilization understands it. Religion in the sense we mean, as *din*,[1] has never really taken root in Western civilization due to its excessive and misguided love of the world and secular life and of man and preoccupation with man's secular destiny. Its inquiring spirit is basically generated in a state of doubt and inner tension; the inner tension is the result of the clash of conflicting elements and opposing values in the sustained dualism, while the doubts maintain the state of inner tension. The state of inner tension in turn produces the insatiable desire to seek and to embark on a perpetual journey of discoveries. The quest is insatiable and the journey perpetual because doubt ever prevails, so that what is sought is never really found, what is discovered never really satisfies its true purpose. It is like the thirsty traveller who at first sincerely sought the water of knowledge, but who later, having found it plain perhaps, proceeded to temper his cup with the salt of doubt so that his thirst now becomes insatiable though he drinks incessantly, and that in thus drinking the water that cannot slake his thirst, he has forgotten the original and true purpose for which the water was sought. The fundamental truths of religion are regarded, in such a scheme of things, as mere theories, or discarded altogether as futile illusions. Absolute

21

values are denied and relative values affirmed; nothing can be certain, except the certainty that nothing can be certain. The logical consequence of such an attitude towards knowledge, which determines and is determined by the world-view, is to negate God and the Hereafter and affirm man and his world. Man is deified and Deity humanized, and the world becomes man's sole preoccupation so that even his own immortality consists in the continuation of his species and his culture in this world. What is called 'change' and 'development' and 'progress' in all their aspects as far as Western civilization is concerned is the result of the insatiable quest and perpetual journey spurred on by doubt and inner tension. The context in which the notions of change and development and progress is understood is always this-worldly, presenting a consistently materialistic world-view that can be termed as a kind of humanistic existentialism. The spirit of Western culture that describes itself as Promethean is like the Camusian Sisyphus who desperately hopes that all is well. I say *desperately hopes* that all is well because I suspect that the fact cannot be that all is well, for I believe that he can never really be truly happy in that state. The pursuit of knowledge, like the struggle to push the Stone from the plains up the Mountain where at the top it is destined to roll down again, becomes a kind of serious *game*, never ceasing, as if to distract the soul from the tragedy of unattainment. No wonder, then, that in Western culture *tragedy* is extolled as being among the noblest values in the *drama* of human existence!

Reliance upon the powers of the human reason alone to guide man through life; adherence to the validity of the dualistic vision of reality and truth; affirmation of the reality of the evanescent-aspect of existence projecting a secular world-view; espousal of the doctrine of humanism; emulation of the allegedly universal reality of drama and tragedy in the spiritual, or transcendental, or inner life of man, making drama and tragedy real and dominant elements in human nature and existence – these elements altogether taken as a whole are, in my opinion, what constitute the substance, the spirit, the character and personality of Western culture and civilization. It is these elements that determine for that culture and civilization the moulding of its concept of knowledge and the direction of its purpose, the formulation of its contents and the systematization of its dissemination; so that the knowledge that is now systematically disseminated throughout the world is not necessarily *true* knowledge, but that which is imbued with the character and personality of Western culture and civilization, and charged with its spirit and geared to its purpose. And it is these elements, then, that must be identified and separated and isolated from the body of knowledge, so that knowledge may be distinguished from what is imbued with these elements, for these elements and what is imbued with them do not represent knowledge as such but they only determine the characteristic form in which knowledge is conceived and evaluated and interpreted in accordance with the purpose aligned to the world-view of Western civilization. It follows too that apart from the identification and separation and isolation of these elements from the body of knowledge, which will no doubt also alter the conceptual forms and values and interpretation of some of the contents of knowledge as it is now presented, its very purpose and system of deployment and dissemination in institutions of learning and in the domain of education must needs be altered accordingly. It may be argued that what is suggested is but *another*, *alternative* interpretation of knowledge imbued with other conceptual forms and values aligned to another purpose which reflects another world-view; and that this being so, and by the same token, what is formulated and disseminated as knowledge might not necessarily reflect *true* knowledge. This, however, remains to be seen, for the test of true knowledge is in man himself, in that if, through an alternative interpretation of knowledge man knows himself and his ultimate destiny, and in thus knowing he achieves happiness, then that knowledge, in spite of its being imbued with certain elements that determine the characteristic form in which it is conceived and evaluated and interpreted in accordance with the purpose aligned to a particular world-view, is true knowledge; for such knowledge has fulfilled man's purpose for knowing.

The Nature of Man

Man has a dual nature, he is both soul and body, he is at once physical being and spirit (15:29; 23:12–14). God taught him *the names* (*al-asma'*) of everything (2:31). By 'the names' we infer that it means *the knowledge* (*al-'ilm*) of everything (*al-ashya'*). This knowledge does not refer to knowledge of the essence (*dhat*) or inmost ground (*sirr*) of a thing (*shay'*) such as, for example, the spirit (*al-ruh*), of which only a *little* knowledge is vouchsafed to man by God (17:85); it refers to knowledge of accidents (sing. *'arad*) and attributes (sing. *sifah*) pertaining to things sensible and intelligible (*mahsusat* and *ma'qulat*) so as to make known the relations and distinctions existing between them and to clarify their natures within these contexts in order to discern and understand their causes, uses, and specific individual purpose. Man is also given *knowledge about* (*ma'rifah*) God, His Absolute Oneness; that God is his true Lord (*rabb*) and true Object of Worship (*ilah*) (7:172; 3:18). The seat of this knowledge in man, both *al-'ilm* and *ma'rifah*, is his spirit or soul (*al-nafs*) and his heart (*al-qalb*) and his intellect (*al-'aql*). In virtue of the fact that man knows (*'arafa*) God in His Absolute Oneness as his true Lord, such knowledge, and the necessary reality of the situation that follows from it, has bound man in a Covenant (*mithaq, 'ahd*) determining his purpose and attitude and action with respect to himself and to God (*q.v.* 7:172*fol.*). This 'binding' and 'determining' of man to a Covenant with God and to a precise nature in regard to his purpose and attitude and action is the binding and determining in religion (*din*) and in real submission (*aslama*) respectively. Thus both *din* and *aslama* are mutual correlates in the nature of man (ref. *fitrah*). Man's purpose is to do *ibadah* to God (51:56), and his duty is obedience (*ta'ah*) to God, which conforms with his essential nature (*fitrah*) created for him by God (*q.v.* 30:30). But man is also 'composed of forgetfulness (*nisyan*);' and he is called *insān* precisely because, having testified to himself the truth of the Covenant, which enjoins obedience to God's Commands and Prohibitions, he *forgot* (*nasiya*) to fulfil his *duty* and *purpose* (*q.v.* narration from ibn 'Abbas:

انما سمى الانسان انسانا لأنه عهد اليه فنسى

with reference to 20:115). Forgetfulness is the cause of man's disobedience, and this blameworthy nature inclines him towards injustice (*zulm*) and ignorance (*jahl*) (33:72). But God has equipped him with the faculties of right vision and apprehension, of real savouring of truth and right speech and communication; and has indicated to him the right and the wrong with respect to the course of action he should take so that he might strive to attain his bright destiny (90:8–10). The choice is left to him. Moreover, God has equipped him with intelligence to know right from wrong and truth from falsehood; and even though his intelligence might confuse him, and provided he is sincere and true to his real nature, God, out of His Bounty and Mercy and Grace will – as He Wills – bestow His guidance (*huda*) upon him to help him attain to truth and right conduct (*q.v.* the supreme example of the Prophet Ibrahim, upon whom be Peace!, in 6:74–82). Man, thus equipped, is

24

meant to be the vicegerent (*khalifah*) of God on earth (2:30), and as such the weighty burden of *trust* (*amanah*) is placed upon him – the trust of responsibility to rule according to God's Will and Purpose and His Pleasure (33:72). The *amanah* implies *responsibility* to be *just* to it; and the 'rule' refers not simply to ruling in the socio-political sense, nor to controlling nature in the scientific sense, but more fundamentally, in its encompassing of the concept *nature* (*tabi'ah*), it refers to the ruling, and governing, and controlling, and maintenance of man by his self. Man also has two souls (*nafsan*) analogous to his dual nature: the higher, rational soul(*al-nafs al-natiqah*); and the lower, animal soul (*al-nafs al-hayawaniyyah*). When God proclaimed the reality of His Lordship to man it is the rational soul that He addressed, so that it is the rational sould that *knows* God. In order for man to fulfil his Covenant with God, to constantly confirm and affirm the Covenant within his total self so that it is enacted as action, as work (*'amal. i.e.* with reference to *ibadah*) performed in obedience to God's Law (*i.e.* the *shari'ah*), the rational soul must assert its supremacy and exert its power and rule over the animal soul, which is subject to it and which must be rendered submissive by it. The effective power and rule exercised by the rational soul over the animal soul is in fact *din*; and the conscious subjugation and total and willing submission of the latter to the former is none other than *aslama* and *islam*. Both *din* and *islam*, leading to excellence in religious conduct (*ihsan*), have to do with the *freedom* of the rational soul, which freedom means the power (*quwwah*) and capacity (*wus'*) to do justice to itself; and this in turn refers to exercise of its rule and supremacy and guidance and maintenance over the animal soul and body. The power and capacity to do justice to itself alludes to its constant affirmation and fulfilment of the Covenant it has sealed with God. *Justice* in Islam is not what refers to a state of affairs which can operate only within a two-person-relation or a dual-party-relation situation, such as: between one man and another; or between the society and the state; or between the king and his subjects. To the question: 'Can one be unjust to one's self?' other religions or philosophies have not given a consistent clear-cut answer. Indeed in Western civilization, for example, though it is true that a man who commits suicide may be considered as committing an unjust act; but this is considered as such insofar only because his suicide deprives the state of the services of a useful citizen, so that his injustice is not to himself, but to the state and society. We say that justice means a harmonious condition or state of affairs whereby every thing is in its right and proper place – such as the cosmos; or similarly, a

25

state of equilibrium, whether it refers to things or living beings. With respect to man, we say that justice means basically a condition and situation whereby he is in his right and proper place. 'Place' here refers not only to his total situation in relation to others, but also to his condition in relation to his self. So the concept of justice in Islam does not only refer to relational situations of harmony and equilibrium existing between one person and another, or between the society and the state, or between the king and his subjects, but far more profoundly and fundamentally so it refers in a primary way to the harmonious and rightly-balanced relationship existing between the man and his self, and in a secondary way only to such as exists between him and another or other, between him and his fellow-men and ruler and king and state and society. Thus to the question: 'Can one be unjust to one's self?' we answer in the affirmative, and add further that justice and injustice indeed *begins* and *ends* with the self. The Holy Quran repeatedly stresses the point that man, when he does wrong, is being unjust (*zalim*) to himself, and that injustice (*zulm*) is a condition wrought by man upon his self (*e.g.* 4:123; 10:44). To understand this we have to refer once again to the soul's Covenant with God and to the fact that man has a dual nature in respect of his two souls and body. The real man can only in fact be his rational soul. If in his existence as a human being he allows his animal or carnal soul to get the better of him and consequently commits acts prohibited by God and displeasing to Him, or if he denies belief in God altogether, then he has thereby repudiated his own affirmation of God's Lordship which he as a rational soul has covenanted with God. He does violence to his own Covenant, his individual contract with God. So just as in the case of one who violates his own contract brings calamity upon himself, in the same way he who does wrong or evil, who disobeys or denies God, violates the contract his soul has made with God, thereby being unjust to his soul. He has also thereby 'lied' – *kadhaba*, another apt Quranic expression – against his own self (soul). It is important in the light of this brief explanation to understand why the belief in the resurrection of bodies is fundamental in Islam, for the soul reconstituted with its former body will not be able to deny what its body has done, for its very eyes, tongue, hands and feet – the organs of ethical and moral conduct – will testify against its acts of injustice to itself (24:24). Though in Islam injustice ostensibly applies between man and God, and between man and man, and between man and his self, in reality, however, injustice is ultimately applicable – even in the two former cases – to man's self alone; in the Islamic world-view

26

and spiritual vision, whether a man disbelieves of disobeys God, or whether he does wrong to another man, it is really to his own self that he does wrong. Injustice, being the opposite of justice, is the putting a thing in a place not its own; it is to misplace a thing; it is to misuse or to wrong; it is to exceed or fall short of the mean or limit; it is to suffer loss; it is deviation from the right course; it is disbelief of what is true, or lying about what is true knowing it to be true. Thus when a man does an act of injustice, it means that he has wronged his own soul, for he has put his soul in a place not its own; he has misused it; he has made it to exceed or fall short of its real nature; he has caused it to deviate from what is right and to repudiate the truth and suffer loss. All that he has thus done – in one way or another – entails a violation of his Covenant with God. It is clear from what we say about injustice that justice implies *knowledge* of the right and proper place for a thing or a being to be; of right as against wrong; of the mean or limit; of spiritual gain as against loss; of truth as against falsehood. And even in the case of knowledge, man has to do justice to it, that is, to know its limit of usefulness and not to exceed or fall short of it; to know its various orders of priority in relation to its usefulness to one's self; to know where to stop and to know what can be gained and what cannot, what is true knowledge in its right place in relation to the knowing one in such wise that what is known produces harmony in the one who knows. To know how to put what knowledge in which place is wisdom (*hikmah*). Other-wise, knowledge without order and seeking it without discipline does lead to confusion and hence to injustice to one's self.

It is clear from the foregoing that in the Islamic political and social organization – be it in one form or another – the man of Islam, the true Muslim, the *khalifatu 'Llah*, is not bound by the social contract, nor does he espouse the doctrine of the Social Contract. Indeed, though he lives and works within the bounds of social polity and authority and contributes his share towards the social good, and though he behaves as *if* a social contract were in force, his is, nevertheless, an *individual contract* reflecting the Covenant his soul has sealed with God; for the Covenant is in reality made for *each* and *every individual* soul. The purpose and end of ethics in Islam is ultimately for the individual; what the man of Islam does here he does in the way he believes to be good only because God and His Messenger say so and he trusts that his actions will find favour with God. Neither the state nor the society are for him real and true objects of his loyalty and obedience, for to him they are not the prerogatives of state and society to the extent that such conduct is due

27

to them as their right; and if he in an Islamic state and society lives and strives for the good of the state and the society, it is only because the society composed of individual men of Islam and the state organized by them set the same Islamic end and purpose as their goal – otherwise he is obliged to oppose the state and strive to correct the errant society and remind them of their true aim in life. We know that in the ultimate analysis man's quest for 'happiness' – as they say in philosophy in connection with ethics – is always for the individual self. It is not the 'happiness' of the collective entity that matters so much more than individual happiness; and every man in reality must indeed think and act for his own salvation, for no other man can be made responsible for his actions since every man bears his own burden of responsibility (6:164). 'Happiness' refers not to the physical entity in man, not to the animal soul and body of man; nor is it a state of mind – it has to do with certainty (*yaqin*) of the ultimate Truth and fulfilment of action in conformity with that certainty; and certainty is a permanent condition referring to what is permanent in man and perceived by his spiritual organ known as the heart (*al-qalb*). It is peace and security and tranquillity of the heart; it is knowledge, and knowledge is belief; it is knowing one's rightful, and hence proper, place in the realm of Creation and one's proper relationship with the Creator: it is a condition known as '*adl* or justice.

Summary of 'review'

We have described most cursorily the bare essentials relating to the nature of man, saying that he is, as it were, a 'double associate': possessed of a dual nature of soul and body, the soul rational and the body animal; that he is at once spirit and physical being, and that he has individuality referred to as the self; that he has attributes reflecting those of his Creator. We say specifically that he has knowledge of the names of things, and knowledge about God; that he has spiritual and rational organs of cognition such as the heart and the intellect; that he has faculties relating to physical, intellectual and spiritual vision an experience; that he has the potentiality to contain within his self guidance and wisdom, and that he has the power and capacity to do justice to his self. We also say that he is forgetful by nature and hence subject to disobedience, injustice and ignorance. In him both qualities, positive and negative, contend for supremacy; but in him also is sealed the means of salvation in true religion and submission. To sum up our brief exposition, we now say that man in his totality is the *locus* (*mahall* or *makan*) in which *din* occurs, and as such he is like a *city* (*madinah*), a state, a cosmopolis. In his real nature he is, as it were, the dweller in his

28

self's city, citizen in his own miniature kingdom. The concept of man as a microcosmic representation (*'alam saghir*) of the macrocosmos (*al-'alam al-kabir*) is most important in relation to knowledge – which is his paramount attribute responsible for the effective establishment of the just order in his self, his being and existence – and to the organization, instruction, inculcation and dissemination of knowledge in his education, specifically with reference to the university, as will be presently outlined.

The Nature of Knowledge

There have been many expositions on the nature of knowledge in Islam, more than in any other religion, culture, and civilization, and this is no doubt due to the preeminent position and paramount role accorded to *al-'ilm* by God in the Holy Quran. These expositions, though apparently varying in substance, encompass the nature of knowledge in its totality. There have been distinctions made between God's Knowledge and the knowledge of man about God, and religion, and the world, and things sensible and intelligible; about spiritual knowledge and wisdom. Thus, for example, knowledge has been understood to mean the Holy Quran; the Revealed Law (Sharia); the Sunnah; Islam; Faith (*iman*); Spiritual Knowledge (*'ilm al-ladunnlyy*), Wisdom (*hikmah*), and Gnosis (*ma'rifah*), also generally referred to as Light; Thought; Science (specific *ilm*, to which the plural: *'ulum* is applied); Education. These expositions range from the earliest periods of Islam to the seventh century after the *Hijrah*, and they include works on exegeses and commentaries of the Holy Quran; commentaries of the Hadith by the compilers of the various *Sihah*; works of the Imams on law and jurisprudence, and those of other foremost jurists specifically concerned with the elucidation of knowledge and discernment; books on knowledge written by various scholars, savants, sages and saints among the Sunnis and Shi'is; expositions by the Mu'tazilah, the Mutakallimun, the Falasifah, the Sufis and the 'ulama' in general; lexicons and dictionaries of technical terminologies in *tasawwuf* and philosophy and the arts or sciences (*al-funun*) by various grammarians, philologists, scholars and men of letters; and in anthologies and other works connected with education and *belles-lettres*.[2] It is generally understood that knowledge requires no definition (*hadd*);[3] that the under-

29

standing of what the concept couched in the term *ilm* means is naturally apprehended by man's knowledge of knowledge, for knowledge is one of his most important attributes, and what it is is already clear to him, so that it dispenses with the need for an explanation describing its specific nature. It is also generally accepted that knowledge can be classified into essential elements, so that its basic classification, insofar as man is concerned, is useful. All knowledge comes from God. For the purpose of classification for our action, we say that in the same manner that man is of a dual nature possessed of two souls, so is knowledge of two kinds: the one is food and life for the soul, and the other is provision with which man might equip himself in the world in his pursuit of pragmatic ends. The first kind of knowledge is given by God through revelation to man; and this refers to the Holy Quran. The Holy Quran is the complete and final Revelation, so that it suffices for man's guidance and salvation; and there is no other knowledge – except based upon it and pointing to it – that can guide and save man. God, however, has never ceased to communicate with man, and out of His Grace, Bounty and Charity He may bestow the favour of specific spiritual knowledge and wisdom upon the elect among His servants – His 'friends' (*i.e.* the *awliya'*) – in proportion to their various degrees of *ihsan* (*q.v.* 10:62, 18:65, 31:12, 38:20). The Holy Quran is *the* knowledge *par excellence*. The Holy Prophet, whom may God Bless and give Peace! – who received the Revelation and brought to man the Holy Quran as it was revealed to him by God, who thus brought to man *the* knowledge, whose own life is the most excellent and perfect interpretation of the Holy Quran so that his life becomes for man the focus of emulation and true guiding spirit – is knowledge of that first knowledge on account of his nature and mission ordained by God. Hence his Sunnah which is his manner of interpreting God's Law Sharia in daily life and practice, is also part of that knowledge. The Sharia is God's Law embodied in the Holy Quran and manifested in word (*qawl*), model action (*fi'il*), and silent confirmation (*taqrir*) in the Sunnah which includes spiritual knowledge and wisdom. So then, the Holy Quran, the *sunnah*, the Sharia, *'ilm al-ladunniyy* and *hikmah* are the essential elements of the first kind of knowledge. As regards the last mentioned – spiritual knowledge and wisdom – man can only receive this through his acts of worship and devotion, his acts of service to God (*ibadat*) which, depending upon God's Grace and his own latent spiritual power and capacity created by God to receive it, the man receives by direct insight or spiritual savouring (*dhawq*) and unveiling to his spiritual vision (*kashf*). This knowledge

30

pertains to his self or soul, and such knowledge (*ma'rifah*) – when experienced in true emulation of the *shari'ah* – gives insight into knowledge of God, and for that reason is the highest knowledge. We are here alluding to knowledge at the level of *ihsan*, where *ibadah* has reached, or rather, has become identified with *ma'rifah* (*q.v.* 51–56 with reference to *li ya'budun* which means, according to the interpretation of ibn 'Abbas: *li ya'rifun*). Since such knowledge ultimately depends upon God's Grace and because it entails deeds and works of service to God as *prerequisites* to its possible attainment, it follows that for it to be received *knowledge of the prerequisites* becomes necessary; and this includes knowledge of the essentials of Islam (*islam – iman – ihsān*), their principles (*arkan*) their meanings and purpose and correct understanding and implementation in everyday life and practice: every Muslim must have knowledge of these prerequisites; must understand the basic essentials of Islam and the Unity of God, His Essence and Attributes (*tawhid*); must have knowledge of the Holy Quran, the Prophet, upon whom be God's Blessings and Peace!, his life and Sunnah, and practise the knowledge thus based in deeds and works of service to God so that every man of Islam be already in the initial stage of that first knowledge, that he be set ready on the Straight Path that leads to God. His further progress along the path of highest virtue (*ihsān*) will depend upon his own knowledge, his own intuitive and speculative power and capacity and performance and sincerity of purpose. The second kind of knowledge refers to knowledge of the sciences (*'ulum*), and is acquired through experience, observation and research; it is discursive and deductive and it refers to objects of pragmatical value. The first kind of knowledge is given by God to man through direct revelation, and the second through speculation and rational effort of enquiry based on his experience of the sensible and intelligible. The first refers to knowledge of objective truths necessary for our guidance, and the second to knowledge of sensible and intelligible data acquired (*kasbi*) for our use and understanding. From the point of view of man, both kinds of knowledge have to be acquired through conscious *action* (*'amal*), for there is no useful knowledge without action resulting from it; and there is no worthwhile action without knowledge. The first knowledge unveils the mystery of Being and Existence and reveals the true relationship between man's self and his Lord, and since for man such knowledge pertains to the ultimate purpose for knowing, it follows that knowledge of its prerequisities becomes the basis and essential foundation for knowledge of the second kind, for knowledge of the latter alone, without the guiding spirit of the

31

former, cannot truly lead man in his life, but only confuses and confounds him and enmeshes him in the labyrinth of endless and purposeless seeking. We also perceive that there is a limit for man even to the first and highest knowledge, whereas no limit obtains in the second kind, so that the possibility of perpetual wandering spurred on by intellectual deception and self-delusion in constant doubt and curiosity is always real. The individual man has no time to waste in his momentary sojourn on earth, and the rightly guided one knows that his individual quest for knowledge of the second kind must needs be limited to his own practical needs and suited to his nature and capacity, so that he may set both the knowledge and himself in their right places in relation to this real self and thus maintain a condition of justice. For this reason and in order to achieve justice as the end, Islam distinguishes the quest for the two kinds of knowledge, making one for the attainment of knowledge of the prerequisites of the first obligatory to all Muslims (*fard 'ayn*), and that of the other obligatory to some Muslims only (*fard kifayah*), and the obligation for the latter can indeed be transferred to the former category in the case of those who deem themselves duty-bound to seek it for their self-improvement. The division in the obligatory quest for knowledge into two catagories is itself a procedure of doing justice to knowledge and to the man who seeks it, for *all* of the knowledge of the prerequisites of the first knowledge is good for man, whereas *not all* of the knowledge of the second kind is good for him, for the man who seeks that latter knowledge, which would bear considerable influence in determining his secular role and position as a citizen, might not necessarily be a *good* man. In Western civilization generally, because its conception of justice is based on secular foundations, it follows that its conception of knowledge is based upon similar foundations, or complementary foundations emphasizing man as a physical entity and a rational animal being, to the extent that it admits of what we have referred to as the second kind of knowledge as the only valid 'knowledge' possible. Consequently, the purpose of seeking knowledge from the lower to the higher levels is, for Western civilization, to produce in the seeker a good citizen. Islam, however, differs in this in that for it the purpose of seeking knowledge is to produce in the seeker a good man. We maintain that it is more fundamental to produce a good man than to produce a good citizen, for the good man will no doubt also be a good citizen, but the good citizen will not necessarily also be a good man. In a sense we say that Islam too maintains that the purpose of seeking knowledge is to produce in the seeker a good citizen, only that we mean by 'citizen' a Citizen of that other Kingdom, so that he acts as such even here and now as a good man. The concept of a 'good man' in Islam connotes not only that he must be 'good' in the general social sense understood, but that he must also first be good to his self, and not be unjust to it in the way we have explained, for if he were unjust to his self, how can he really be just to others? Thus we see that already in this most fundamental concept in life – the concept of knowledge – Islam is at variance with Western civilization, in that for Islam (a) knowledge includes faith and belief (*iman*); and that (b) the purpose for seeking knowledge is to inculcate goodness or justice in man as man and individual self, and not merely in man as citizen or integral part of society: it is man's value as real man, as the dweller in his self's city, as citizen in his own microcosmic kingdom, as spirit, that is stressed, rather than his value as a physical entity measured in terms of the pragmatic or utilitarian sense of his usefulness to state and society and the world.

As the philosophical basis for the purpose and aims of education, and for the establishment of an integrated core-knowledge in the educational system, it seems to me important to state the essential character of the Islamic vision of Reality. The Islamic vision of Reality is no other than the philosophical core of Islam which determines its world-view. Islam focuses its religious and philosophical vision (*shuhud*) of Reality and its world-view on Being, and distinguishes between Being (*wujud*) and Existence (*mawjud*); between Unity (*wahdah*) and Multiplicity (*kathrah*); between Subsistence (*baqa*) and Evanescence (*fana'*). This vision of Reality is based upon revealed knowledge through religious experience, and embraces both the objective, metaphysical and ontological reality as well as the subjective, mystical and psychological experience of that reality. Phenomenologically Islam, in confirmation of its vision of Reality, affirms 'being' rather than 'becoming' or 'coming-into-being', for the Object of its vision is clear, established, permanent and unchanging. This confirmation and affirmation is absolute because it springs from the certainty (*yaqin*) or revealed knowledge; and since its Object is clear and established and permanent and unchanging, so likewise is Islam, together with its way of life and method of practice and values, an absolute reflection of the mode of the Object. Thus Islam itself is like its Object in that it emulates its ontological nature as subsisting and unchanging – as being; and hence affirms itself to be complete and perfect as confirmed by God's words in the Holy Quran (5:4) and it denies the possibility of ever being in need of completion or evolution towards perfection; and such concepts as *development* and *progress* and *perfection* when applied to man's life and history and destiny must indeed refer, in Islam, ultimately to the spiritual and real nature of man. If this were not so, then it can never really mean, for Islam, *true* development and progress and perfection, as it would mean only the development and progress and perfection of the animal in man; and that would not be his true evolution unless such evolution realizes in him his true nature as spirit.

Progress

Change, development and *progress*, according to the Islamic viewpoint, refer to the return to the genuine Islam enunciated and practised by the Holy Prophet (may God bless and give him peace!) and his noble Companions and their Followers (blessings and peace be upon them all!) and the faith and practice of genuine Muslims after them; and they also refer to the self and mean its return to its original nature and religion (Islam). These concepts pertain to presupposed situations in which Muslims find themselves, as is the case today, going astray and steeped in ignorance of Islam being confused and unjust to their nature. In such situations, their endeavour to re-direct themselves back onto the Straight and True Path and to return to the condition of genuine Islam – such endeavour, which entails change, is development; and such return, which consists in development, is progress. Thus, for Islam, the process of movement towards genuine Islam by Muslims who have strayed away from it is development; and such development is the only one that can truly be termed as progress. Progress is neither 'becoming' or 'coming-into-being', nor movement towards that which is 'coming-into-being' and never becomes 'being' for the notion of 'something aimed at', or the 'goal' inherent in the concept 'progress' can only contain real meaning when it refers to that which is already *clear* and permanently *established*, already *being*. Hence what is already clear and established, already in the state being, cannot suffer change, nor is it subject to constant slipping from the grasp of achievement, nor constantly receding beyond attainment. The term 'progress' reflects a *definite direction* that is aligned to a *final purpose* that is meant to be achieved in life; if the direction sought is still vague, still coming-into-being, as it were, and the purpose aligned to it is not final, then how can involvement in it truly mean progress? Those who grope in the dark cannot be referred to as progressing, and they who say such people are progressing have merely uttered a lie against the true meaning and purpose of progress, and they have lied unto their selves! (*q.v.* 2:17–20)

The Islamic world-view is not to be construed as a dualism, for

34

although two elements are involved, yet the one is dependent and subsistent while the other is dependent upon it; the one is absolute and the other relative; the one is real and the other a manifestation of that reality. So there is only One Reality and Truth, and all Islamic values pertain ultimately to it alone, so that to the Muslim, individually and collectively, all endeavour towards change and development and progress and perfection is invariably determined by the world-view that projects the vision of the One Reality and confirms the affirmation of the same Truth. In affirmation of Being, the Holy Quran, the source of Islam and projector of the Islamic world-view and the vision of the One Reality and Truth, is the expression of the finality and perfection of 'being' just as Islam is the phenomenological affirmation of 'being'; and he who conveyed the Holy Quran to mankind himself represents the finality and perfection of 'being' in man, may God bless and give him peace!

In the same way that the Islamic vision of Reality is centred on Being, so is that Being viewed in Islam as a Hierarchy from the highest to the lowest. Within this context is also seen the relationship between man and the universe, his position in the order of Being and his analogical description as a microcosm reflecting the Macrocosm without the reverse being the case. Knowledge is also ordered hierarchically, and our task at present is to alter the system of education known to us – and in some cases to modify it – so that it patterns itself after the Islamic system of order and discipline.

Definition and Aims of Education

We have said that justice implies knowledge, which also means that knowledge is prior to justice. We have defined justice as a harmonious condition or state of affairs whereby every thing or being is in its right and proper place – such as the cosmos; or similarly, a state of equilibrium, whether it refers to things or living beings. We said further that, in respect of man and in view of his dual nature, justice is a condition and situation whereby he is in his right and proper place – the situation in relation to others, and the condition in relation to his self. Then we mentioned that the knowledge of the 'right place' for a thing or a being to be is wisdom. Wisdom is a God-given knowledge enabling the one in whom the knowledge subsists to apply the knowledge in such wise that it (i.e. the application or judgement) causes the occurrence of justice.

35

Justice is then the existential condition of wisdom manifested in the sensibilia and intelligibilia and in the spiritual realm in respect of the two souls of man. The external manifestation of justice in life and society is none other than the occurrence within it of *adab*. I am using the concept (*ma'na*) of *adab* here in the early sense of the term, before the innovations of the literary geniuses. *Adab* in the original basic sense is the *inviting to a banquet*. The idea of a *banquet* implies that the host is a man of *honour* and *prestige*, and that *many* people are present; that the people who are present are those who in the host's estimation are deserving of the honour of the invitation, and they are therefore people of refined qualities and upbringing who are expected to behave as befits their station, in speech, conduct and etiquette. In the same sense that the enjoyment of fine food in a banquet is greatly enhanced by noble and gracious company, and that the food be partaken of in accordance with the rules of refined conduct, behaviour and etiquette, so is knowledge to be extolled and enjoyed, and approached by means of conduct as befits its lofty nature. And this is why we said analogically that knowledge is the *food* and *life* of the soul. In virtue of this, *adab* also means to *discipline* the *mind* and *soul*; it is acquisition of the *good qualities* and *attributes* of mind and soul; it is to *perform* the *correct* as against the erroneous *action*, of *right* as against wrong; it the *preserving from disgrace*. The analogy of invitation to banquet to partake of fine food, and to knowledge to imbue the intellect and soul with sustenance from it is significantly and profoundly expressed in a *hadith* narrated by ibn Mas'ud, may God be well pleased with him!:

ان هذا القرآن مأدبة اللّه في الأرض فتعلموا من مأدبته

The *Lisan al-'Arab* says that *ma'dabat* means *mad'at* (1:206:2) so that the Holy Quran is God's invitation to a spiritual banquet on earth, and we are exhorted to partake of it by means of acquiring real knowledge of it. Ultimately, real knowledge of it is the 'tasting of its true flavour' – and that is why we said earlier, with reference to the essential elements of the first kind of knowledge, that man receives spiritual knowledge and wisdom from God by direct insight or spiritual savouring (*dhawq*), the experience of which almost simultaneously unveils the reality and truth of the matter to his spiritual vision (*kashf*). He in whom *adab* inheres reflects wisdom; and with respect to society *adab* is the deployment of the just order within it. *Adab*, then, is the spectacle (*mashhad*) of justice as it is reflected by wisdom; and it is the acknowledgement and recognition of the various hierarchies (*maratib*) in the order of being and

36

existence and knowledge, and concomitant action in accord with the acknowledgement and recognition. Education is the instilling and inculcation of *adab* in man – it is *ta'dib*. Thus *adab* is precisely what applies to man if he must acquit himself successfully and well in this life and the Hereafter. And the definition of education and its aims and purpose are already in fact contained in the brief exposition of the concept of *adab* as here outlined.

Islamic System of Order and Discipline

We referred earlier to an Islamic system of order and discipline. Islam itself is the epitome of the Divine cosmic order and discipline, and the man who is conscious of his destiny in Islam knows that in like manner he too is an order and discipline, in that he is like a city, a kingdom in miniature; for in him as in all mankind, is manifested the Attributes of the Creator without the reverse being the case. Man knows that he is knowing, and experience of such knowledge tells him that he is at once being and existence; a unity and yet a multiplicity, subsistent and at the same time evanescent – he is on the one hand *permanent*, and on the other *change*. His personality from his birth till his death as a phenomenal being remains unchanged, even though his physical being is ever-changing and suffers final dissolution. And this is due to the fact that his personality refers to the permanent in him – his rational soul. Were it not for this quality or permanence, it would not be possible for knowledge to inhere in him. Thus the knowledge of the first kind, which is his life and food, refers to his rational soul; and his education as a whole and quest for knowledge leading to the first kind of knowledge, in so far as his personality is concerned, entails the pursuit of knowledge of the prerequisites to that first knowledge (*i.e.* the *fard 'ayn*). In view of the permanent nature of his personality, so is education in Islam a continuous process throughout his life on earth, and it covers every aspect of that life. From the point of view of linguistic usage, we must see that the fact that the term *'ilm* has been applied in Islam to encompass the totality of life – the spiritual, intellectual, religious, cultural, individual and social – means that its character is universal, and that it is necessary to guide man to his salvation. No other culture and civilization has ever applied a single term for knowledge to encompass all activities in man's life. Perhaps this was why the organization, inculcation and

37

dissemination of knowledge was conceived as a system of order and discipline pertaining to the *kulliyyah*, a concept conveying the idea of the *universal*. We know that from the earliest periods Islam began its educational system significantly with the mosque as its centre; and with the mosque (*Jami*) continuing to be its centre even – in some cases – till the present day, there developed other educational institutions such as the *maktab*; the *bayt al-hikmah*; the gatherings of scholars and students (*majalis*); the *dar al-'ulum*, and the *madaris*; and in the fields of medicine, astronomy and devotional sciences there rose the hospitals, observatories, and zawiyah within the Sufi fraternities. We also know that the early Western universities were modelled after the Islamic originals. Very little information is available to me, however, concerning the original concept of the university within the Islamic system of education, and the extent to which original Islamic concepts pertaining to the structure of the university had influenced the Western copies. But the general character and structure of the universities today, which are veritable copies of Western models, still reveal significant traces of their Islamic origin. The very name for the institution which derives from Latin: *universitatem* clearly reflects the original Islamic *kulliyyah*. Then again, apart from the role of medicine in Islamic learning and its early and great influence in the West, the anatomical concept of the *faculty*, which harks back on *quwwah* which refers to a *power inherent in the body of an organ*, is most significant, not only – it seems to me – in establishing its Islamic origin, but in demonstrating the fact that since the concept 'faculty' refers to a living being in whom the attribute 'knowledge' subsists, and that this knowledge is the governing principle determining his thought and action, the university must have been conceived in emulation of the general structure, in form function and purpose, of man. It was meant to be a microcosmic representation of man – indeed, of the Universal Man (*al-insān al-kulliyy*).

But the university as it later was developed in the West and emulated today all over the world no longer reflects man. Like a man with no personality, the modern university has no abiding, vital centre, no permanent underlying principle establishing its final purpose. It still pretends to contemplate the universal and even claims to possess faculties and departments as if it were the body of an organ – but it has no brain, let alone intellect and soul, except only in terms of a purely administrative function of maintenance and physical development. Its development is not guided by a *final* principle and definite purpose, except by the relative principle urging on the pursuit of knowledge

38

incessantly, with no absolute end in view. It is a symbol that has become ambiguous – unlike the Quranic concept of *ayah* – because it points to itself (*i.e.* to the sciences for the sake of the sciences) instead of to what it is meant to represent (*i.e.* to man), and hence is productive of perpetual confusion and even scepticism. Because of the secular basis of Western culture, which is mentioned in the beginning, the university is geared to a secular *relative* purpose, and hence reflects the secular *state* and *society* and not the universal *man*. But there never has been nor ever will be, except in Islam in the person of the Holy Prophet, upon whom be God's Blessings and Peace!, the Universal Man (*al-insān al-kamil*) that can be reflected in microcosmic representation as 'university'. Neither can state nor society be truly considered as capable of possessing an attribute called knowledge, for that is only possessed by the individual man. And even if it be argued that the modern university is in fact emulating man, yet it is the secular man that is portrayed; the rational animal devoid of soul, like a circle with no centre. The various faculties and departments within them, like the various faculties and senses of the body, have in the modern university become uncoordinated, each preoccupied with its own endless pursuits; each exercising its own 'free will', as it were, and not the coherent will of one being, for there is no 'being' – all is 'becoming'. Can one be judged sane and coherent who contemplates some matter, and at the same time recognizes something else entirely different from what is being contemplated and who says something again quite different altogether, who hears different sounds and sees yet again different things? The modern university is the epitome of man in a condition of *zulm*, and such a condition is maintained by the encouragement and elevation and legitimization of doubt and conjecture as epistemological tools of scientific enquiry. The Holy Quran repeatedly repudiates such methods, branding them contraries of knowledge. Thus doubt (*shakk*), conjecture and guess (*zann*), disputation and contention (*mira'*, i.e. *jadala*), inclination of the mind or animal soul towards natural desire (*hawa*), are all generally considered blameworthy – the more so when applied to, and masquerading as, knowledge. We must take note of the significance that, in the case of Western culture and civilization, and with reference ot the sociology of knowledge, the West has defined knowledge in terms of the effort of science as control of nature and society. With respect to man as an individual, to the improvement and identification and elevation of his personality and the desire to learn about the Divine order of the world and salvation, to this most important *purpose* – and

39

hence true nature of knowledge – the West no longer attaches any significance and reality. This is and has been so by virtue of the fact that the West acknowledges no single Reality to fix its vision on; no single, valid scripture to confirm and affirm in life; no single human Guide whose words and deeds and actions and entire mode of life can serve as model to emulate in life, as the Universal Man. We cannot, as Muslims, afford to overlook this important fact; for Islam embodies within itself all the three fundamentals of knowledge and action mentioned above, and for that reason alone classifies knowledge into two kinds and clarifies the concept of the knowledge of prerequisites (*fard 'ayn*) that *must* form the basic core of all education. The following simple diagrams will help summarize in bare figurative framework the main subject of this paper:

Fig. 1: Man

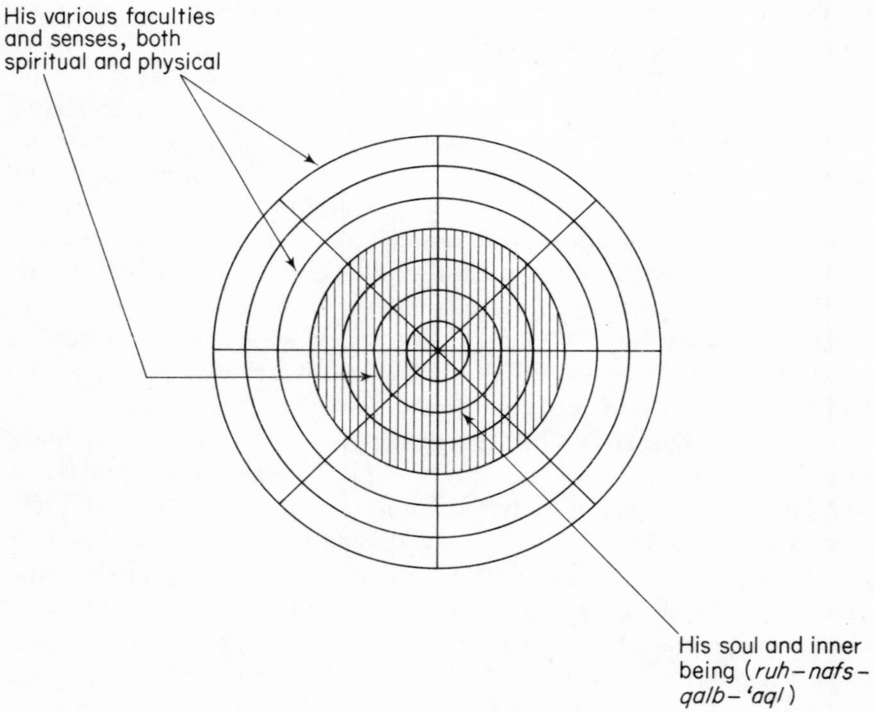

His various faculties and senses, both spiritual and physical

His soul and inner being (*ruh – nafs – qalb – 'aql*)

Fig. 2: Knowledge (Man's)

Knowledge of Sciences represents the *Fard Kifayah* knowledge whose parts have been deployed according to priorities of service to state and society in the Muslim community

Knowledge of Prerequisites to Revealed Knowledge represents the *Fard 'Ayn* knowledge whose parts have been integrated to form the *core* knowledge of individuals in Islamic education

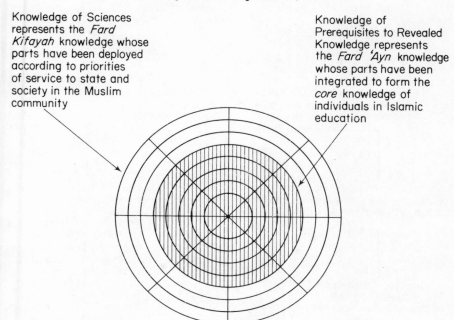

Fig. 3: The Islamic University
(as microcosmic representation of the Universal
Man in terms of knowledge)

Knowledge of Sciences: its various faculties and departments corresponding to man's physical faculties and senses

Knowledge of Prerequisites (*Fard 'Ayn*) must reflect inner being of man (*ruh—nafs—qalb— 'aql*) and his spiritual senses in terms of faculties and departments. Must contain *specialization*

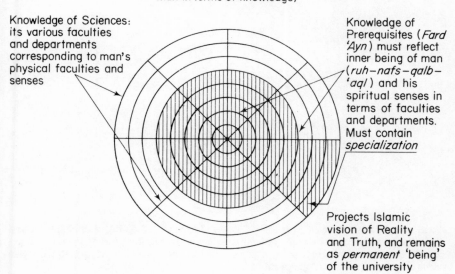

Projects Islamic vision of Reality and Truth, and remains as *permanent* 'being' of the university

41

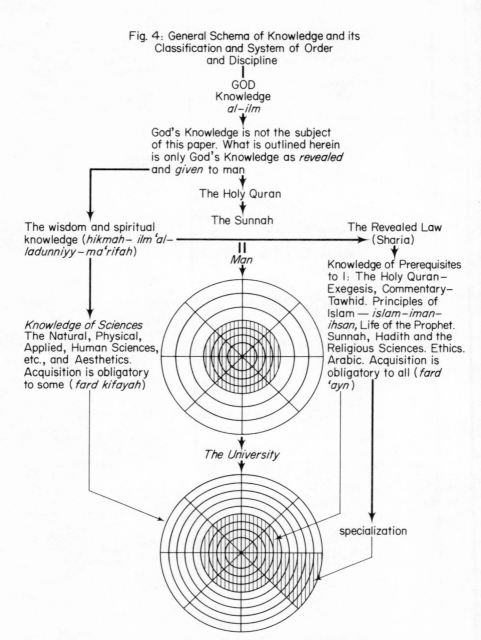

Fig. 4: General Schema of Knowledge and its
Classification and System of Order
and Discipline

GOD
Knowledge
al-ilm

God's Knowledge is not the subject
of this paper. What is outlined herein
is only God's Knowledge as *revealed*
and *given* to man

The Holy Quran

The Sunnah

The wisdom and spiritual
knowledge (*hikmah– ilm'al–
ladunniyy–ma'rifah*)

II
Man

The Revealed Law
(Sharia)

Knowledge of Prerequisites
to I: The Holy Quran–
Exegesis, Commentary–
Tawhid. Principles of
Islam — *islam–iman–
ihsan,* Life of the Prophet.
Sunnah, Hadith and the
Religious Sciences. Ethics.
Arabic. Acquisition is
obligatory to all (*fard
'ayn*)

Knowledge of Sciences
The Natural, Physical,
Applied, Human Sciences,
etc., and Aesthetics.
Acquisition is obligatory
to some (*fard kifayah*)

The University

specialization

Note: With respect to the system of order and discipline in the educational sphere, the above Schema descends to the university, which is the highest level of the education system. However, the same pattern as outlined for the university applies to the lower levels in gradations from the lowest to the highest.

Concluding Remarks and Suggestions

In the foregoing pages, I have attempted to elucidate certain *key concepts* pertaining to the nature and purpose of knowledge from the Islamic viewpoint, and to demonstrate the fundamental nature of their mutual interrelation and interdependence. These key concepts must form the essential elements of the Islamic system of education. They are:

1. The concept of religion (*dīn*);
2. The concept of man (*insān*);
3. The concept of knowledge (*ilm* and *ma'rifah*);
4. The concept of wisdom (*hikmah*);
5. The concept of justice (*'adl*);
6. The concept of right action (*'amal* as *adab*);
7. The concept of the university (*kulliyyah-jami'ah*).

In terms of practical application, the first refers to the *purpose* of seeking knowledge and involvement in the process of education; the second to the *scope*; the third to the *content*; the fourth to the *criteria* in relation to the second and third; the fifth to the *deployment* in relation to the fourth; the sixth to the *method* in relation to the first down to the fifth; and the seventh to the *form of implementation* in relation to all that precedes it.

In appraising the present situation with regard to the formulation and dissemination of knowledge in the Muslim world, we must see that infiltration of key concepts from the Western world has brought confusion which will ultimately cause grave consequences if left unchecked. Since what is formulated and disseminated in and through universities and other institutions of learning from the lower to the higher levels is in fact knowledge *infused* with the character and personality of Western culture and civilization and *moulded* in the crucible of Western culture (see *Introduction*), our task will be first to *isolate the elements* including the key concepts which make up that culture and civilization (see the last paragraph of the *Introduction*). These elements and key concepts are mainly prevalent in that branch of knowledge pertaining to the human sciences, although it must be noted that even in the natural, physical and applied sciences, particularly where they deal with *interpretation of facts* and *formulation of theories*, the same process of isolation of the elements and key concepts should be applied; for the interpretations and formulations indeed belong to the sphere of the human sciences. The 'Islamization' of present-day knowledge means precisely that, *after* the isolation process referred to, the knowledge free of the elements and key concepts isolated are *then* infused with the Islamic elements and key concepts, which, in view of their fundamental nature as defining the *fitrah*, in fact imbue the knowledge with the quality of its natural function and purpose and thus makes it *true* knowledge. It will not do to accept present-day knowledge as it is, and then hope to 'islamize' it merely by 'grafting' or 'transplanting' into it Islamic sciences and principles; this method will but produce conflicting results not altogether beneficial nor desirable. Neither 'grafting' nor 'transplant' can produce the desired result when the 'body' is already possessed by foreign elements and consumed by disease. The foreign elements and disease will have first to be drawn out and neutralized before the body of knowledge can be remoulded in the crucible of Islam.

Our next important task will be the formulation and integration of the essential Islamic elements and key concepts so as to produce a composition which will comprise the core knowledge to be deployed in our educational system from the lower to the higher levels in respective gradations designed to conform to the standard of each level. The core knowledge at the university level, which must first be formulated before that at any level, must be composed of ingredients pertaining to the nature of man (*insān*); the nature of religion (*dīn*) and man's involvement in it; of knowledge (*ilm* and *ma'rifah*), wisdom (*hikmah*) and justice (*'idl*) with respect to man and his religion; the nature of right action (*'amal-adab*). These will have to be referred to the concept of God, His Essence and Attributes (*tawhid*); the Revelation (the Holy Quran), its meaning and message; the Revealed Law (*shari'ah*) and what necessarily follows: the Prophet (upon whom be God's Blessings and Peace!), his life and *sunnah*, and the history and message of the Prophets before him. They will also have to be referred to knowledge of the Principles and practice of Islam, the religious sciences (*'ulum al-shar'iyyah*), which must include legitimate elements of *tasawwuf* and Islamic philosophy, including valid cosmological doctrines pertaining to the hierarchy of being, and knowledge of Islamic ethics and moral principles and *adab*. To this must be added knowledge of the Arabic language and of the Islamic world-view as a whole. This core knowledge, integrated and composed as a harmonious unity and designed at the university level as a model structure and content for the other levels, must invariably be reflected in successively simpler forms at the secondary and primary levels of the educational system. At each level, the core knowledge must be designed to be made identical for application in the educational

44

system throughout the Muslim world, since the core knowledge is obligatory to all Muslims (*fard 'ayn*).

With respect to the knowledge of the sciences designated as obligatory to some only (*fard kifayah*), it has been pointed out that it must be imbued with the Islamic elements and key concepts *after* the foreign elements and key concepts have been isolated from its every branch. To this knowledge must be added the knowledge of Islamic history, culture and civilization, Islamic thought, and the development of the sciences in Islam. In this category too new courses on comparative religion from the Islamic point of view, on Western culture and civilization, must be designed as a means for Muslims to understand the culture and civilization that has been and is and will continue to be confronting Islam. Knowledge of all these will assure logical continuity in the successive educational progression from the core knowledge to that of the sciences. Many new subjects will undoubtedly be added to the above. The determining of the order of priority, with reference to individual striving after the various branches of the knowledge of the sciences, will invariably depend on its relative usefulness and benefit to self, society, and state respectively. The formulation of the concept of 'relative usefulness and benefit to self, society and state' must be contained in the form of general principles reflecting the Islamic elements and key concepts. It follows that the order of priority with reference to choice must not be left to the judgement of individuals, but must likewise be planned to conform with the current needs of the self-society-state, which is none other than those of the Community. Whereas in the case of the core knowledge the obligation to acquire it is directed to all and to both sexes, in the case of knowledge of the sciences, certain branches may not be deemed appropriate for females; so that some may be obligatory to males only and some to females. Regarding entrance into the higher levels of education, it is not sufficient merely for an individual to be allowed to qualify on the basis of good results in formal scientific subjects, as is practised today everywhere. No doubt personal conduct is recognized as important in many educational systems, but their notions of personal conduct are vague and not really applied effectively in education, and no objective system has been devised to determine the nature of those elements of human conduct and behaviour that are undesirable for purposes of higher learning leading to appointments to responsible posts and offices. It is neither impossible nor impracticable to devise a system for implementation into the educational framework whereby certain individuals can be debarred

45

from higher education. Knowledge (*i.e.* the *fard kifayah*) is not necessarily everyone's right; no one in Islam has the right to do wrong – this would be a contradiction in terms and purpose. To do wrong is injustice, and this not a *right*. The doing something wrong that is considered in Islam to be the most destructive to self, society, and state revolves around three vices: lying, breaking a promise, and betraying a trust. The Holy Quran is most emphatic in denouncing these vices as they are vices which caused man's downfall and which man not only perpetrates on his fellow-man, but even on God Himself! Hence the profound significance of the *hadith* narrated by Abu Hurayrah, may God be well pleased with him! concerning the mark of the hypocrite, that when he speaks, he lies; and when he promises, he breaks the promise; and when he is entrusted with something he betrays the trust (اذا حدث كذب واذا وعد خلف واذا اتتمن خان). I say that this well-known *hadith* is of profound significance not only because it states in succinct summary the precise nature of the most destructive of man's vices, but also because it furnishes us with clear indication of the criteria to be adopted when judging human character and conduct. I believe that the *hadith* is not meant to be heeded simply as wise counsel whose application is to be left to individual judgement and responsibility, but that it must be seriously systematized into an educational device which can be applied as a moral check on all who will pass through the educational process. Such a device, applied positively and effectively through the levels of the educational system, will assist in minimizing the emergence and perpetration in Muslim society, state and leadership, of betrayal of trust leading to injustice and ignorance.

The scope and limited duration set for this paper do not permit us to go into details. This paper is meant to set forth a statement of the problem and a possible and acceptable solution to it; to gather together the key concepts and explain them in the correct Islamic perspective. If at all my humble attempt to meet the demands of this task in any small way contributes to the true and the correct answer, then to God alone the Praise, for every atom of good is accomplished through His help and guidance.

The details of the formulation and integration of the core knowledge, the order of deployment of the knowledge of the sciences in the academic structure and in the priority framework in the system of order and discipline, will have to be methodically set forth for thorough research by a team of expert scholars and thinkers experienced in academic administration. This team should be gathered together in one place where recourse to the necessary facilities can conveniently be had, and where consultations, discussions and research among the members can be facilitated and coordinated without undue expenditure of human and financial resources, and in time. The blueprint for the above proposed concept and for the restructuring of the academic and administrative system according to priorities can then be prepared in a few years. When this is accomplished, the experimental stage, beginning with the university, can commence operations. Naturally, the assistance and support of any wise and far-sighted Muslim government desirous of achieving the results of this long-term but realistic project is urgently sought, both at the initial stage of research and preparation of the blueprint, and at the experimental stage of setting up the Islamic university. This might take several years of critical assessment and appraisal of the effectiveness of its planned implementation, and will involve evaluation of at least the first intake of graduates; of methodical analysis and correction of errors in the process of perfecting the system until it is found to be satisfactory. When this stage has been achieved, the system can then be recommended to the Muslim world at large, and the follow-up in connection with the lower levels of the educational system can be planned and implemented after the pattern of the university has been perfected. It is futile to attempt short-term myopic measures in providing a solution to a problem of this magnitude. Our great and God-fearing predecessors of astute vision and profound intellectual and spiritual depth, have laboured in terms of centuries to build splendid systems of thought and action with God's help and guidance, and if we are even to hope to rise to the same expectation, then we must humbly emulate their example.

Chapter Two

The Role of Religion in Education

Muhammad Qutb

Muhammad Qutb, Professor of Islamics and Comparative Religion at King Abdulaziz University, Mecca, was born in Assyout, Egypt in 1919. Formerly he was the Director of the Bureau of One thousand Book Translation Project in Egypt and a member of the Muslim Brotherhood of Egypt for which he was jailed by Nasr for seven years. He is a prolific writer in Arabic and one of the most influential Arabic thinkers of today. His publications include: *Man between Materialism and Islam*; *Islam the Misunderstood Religion*; *Man and Society*; *Selection from the Prophet's Guidance*; *Conflict in Traditions and Conventions*; *Islamic Educational Methodology*; *Are We Muslims? Method of Islamic Arts*; *Studies in Human Psychology*; *Permanence and Change in Human Life*; *Twentieth Century Jahiliyya*; three volumes on *Tawhid* for Saudi schools.

When we talk about religious education, the formal and the traditional lessons on religion immediately come to mind. And even if our imagination flew beyond the normal limits of the rigid religious lesson, it would seize on a sermon or a religious speech, not more, and there it would come to a halt. We do not, in fact, impart education in our schools, particularly Islamic education.

If the schools set up in most parts of the Moslem world are reluctant to carry out religious education, or if they are willing to adopt it but do not know how, the final result is the same in either case – we do not, in actual fact, bring our children up according to the ideals of true Islamic education. The impact of the genuine Islamic spirit on our school curricula is hardly noticeable. We ought to consider, however, that a formal and traditional lesson on religion will not be sufficient to meet the desired human requirements, particularly in contemporary life. An overdose of a religious speech or sermon would, instead of rendering religion pleasant, interesting and likeable, create a repellent and damaging effect. We ourselves must be frank and state openly and unequivocally the fact that religion is now utterly isolated and alienated from our lives and feelings because we do not practise it in reality. In most parts of the Muslim world, we do not resort to the Sharia nor do our life-governing laws draw upon it. Our lives, on the whole, are not patterned on Allah's Curriculum which comprises belief, duties of

48

worship, work, feeling, conduct, politics, economics, sociology . . . etc.; in fact it encompasses life and the hereafter in one self-contained discipline. But our concepts and approaches, our feelings and thoughts, our morals and modes of behaviour are not derived from Islam. The vast majority of those things have reached us from here and there, from every corner of the world where Islam is unheard of and not believed in. Religion, as we feel and approach it now, has dwindled from the integrated inclusiveness known to earlier Muslim generations into something more or less akin to the Western ecclesiastical approach, namely, an emotional relationship between Lord and servant outside the sphere of actual life. This fact, which we ought to acknowledge frankly and unequivocally if we are to deal with our subject honestly and seriously, casts its thick and impenetrable shadow over our entire lives; besides, it is closely relevant to education curricula.

Earlier Muslim generations built their communities on religious education which was the core and the essence. The Sharia was the life-governing law. Islamic morals and modes of behaviour were predominant. To put it in a nutshell, Islam disciplined and governed the lives of people in those earlier Muslim communities. Religious education was carried out both at home and at school, in the mosque and in the street and through all communications media. Formal lessons on religion became relevant in this context since they were entirely devoted to giving every individual Muslim instructions about his belief, duties of worship, dealings, and impositions whether at home or in the mosque. The formal lesson on religion, in that sense, did not have to reinforce religious education; that job was undertaken by other media, particularly the home and the family at uninterrupted times and not during the limited periods allotted to formal lessons.

To make Allah's doctrine rule supreme is, in itself, a self-contained sound educational system to which the entire human race should be brought up. Saying one's prayers at appointed times is extremely educative. Consolidating and intensifying Islamic patterns of conduct among children would help them adhere to Islamic morals and education. The sight of a God-fearing woman wholly committed to the divine word of Allah, or a man taking his words, steps, work and duties of worship seriously – is a type of education which, in the presence of a good model, leaves its indelible mark on a child's behaviour.

Once all these types of education are available – we have cited a few specimens by way of illustration – it is neither strange nor objectionable to have a formal lesson on religion wholly concerned with giving

49

religious information without necessarily paying the least heed to basic education. We could rest assured that the desired education would be given everywhere outside the limited scope and time of a formal classroom lesson. The sole and basic objective of the lesson would then be to inculcate religious beliefs and instil them in the minds of the young. It is an undeniable fact that our hold on religion has now weakened. Religion has gradually been banished from our minds and hearts. The home and the street, instead of promoting religious education, have on the contrary combined to undermine it. In such a deplorable state nothing remains available except school curricula and channels of information through which religious education can be promoted and intensified. When such is the case, would a lesson given in the classroom or the mosque be sufficient as a lesson crammed with rigid disconnected bits of information assembled according to the planning of centuries ago? The formal lesson as such, the sermon and the religious speech, are rather like a fine building that has once been and is now gone. It has collapsed, leaving behind a few stones to remind us of the gigantic walls that once stood. Would those stones rebuild the fine gigantic structure that was once erected?

In fact the picture is far worse than that. To summarize what has been mentioned so far, let us say that since the educational institutions relinquished their role and the entire heavy burden of providing information has been placed on educational curricula and the mass media, the formal lesson on religion, the sermon or the religious talk has proved utterly insufficient and futile in so far as religious education is concerned. What wonder then if the atmosphere of a formal lesson at school, or a sermon or a religious talk on radio and T.V. is far from being religious and very often irreligious? I am not going to talk about the means of information but will concentrate only on educational curricula. Outside the four walls of an ordinary classroom, where a formal lesson on religion is given, one cannot feel that one is in an Islamic school or Islamic university. It will be soon found that the materials taught and the teaching methods are not very dissimilar from those in the Western world, a world absolutely anti-religious though it hides its anti-religious nature behind the curtain of secularism and claims that it is only non-religious and not anti-religious.

Of course, we are well aware of the circumstances in which Europe lived from the Rennaissance onwards. These circumstances have made the gap between science and religion extremely wide. People classed religion as different from science, and created a hideous antagonism between them. The word Allah (Praise be to Him), if mentioned in a piece of scientific research, would have been considered very objectionable. It would have, in their view, contaminated the whole research. Darwin said in one of his books, it would 'introduce a supernatural element into a purely mechanical position'. Europeans have their own justifications concerning this matter, for Allah says in the Holy Writ:

'Nay, man will be evidence against himself, even though he were to put up his excuses.' (Sura *The Resurrection*, verses 14–15).

What excuses do we Muslims offer if we imitate the Europeans and differentiate, as they do, between science and religion? Science and religion exist side by side within man's innate nature. No contradiction or enmity has ever been created between them. Paying homage to God and worshipping Him in awe is naturally human; 'When thy Lord drew forth from the children of Adam – from their loins – their descendants, and made them testify concerning themselves, (saying): "Am I not your Lord (who cherishes and sustains you)?" – They said: "Yes"' (Sura *A'raf*, verse 172). The desire to know everything about the universe and to utilize its infinite resources in the interest of man is naturally human.

Man's insatiable desire for the acquisition of knowledge was intended to help him inherit and inhabit the earth. 'And He taught Adam the nature of all things.' (Sura *Baqara*, verse 31). 'And He has subjected to you, as from Him, all that is in the heavens and on earth.' (Sura *Jatiya* verse 13). 'Proclaim! And thy Lord is Most Bountiful, – He Who taught (The use of) the Pen, – taught man that which he knew not.' (Sura *Alaq*, verses 3–5). In a sound human nature there is no contradiction between these two innate tendencies; for the one helps man to commit himself wholly to the divine word of God and address Him in awe through duties of worship while the other leads man to the acquisition of knowledge of God's names, characteristics and actions in this universe. This will eventually culminate in more God-fearing and God-worshipping. 'Those truly fear God, among His servants, who have knowledge.' (Sura *Fatir*, verse 28).

Only the '*jahilliyyats*' (agnostics predominant before the advent of Islam) separate these two integrated and intertwined dispositions. Contemporary European agnosticism, in particular, creates enmity and hatred between them. The Islamic school; primary, preparatory, secondary or university, shall not and must not commit this deadly sin and isolate science from religion. Science should not be taught without religion and vice versa.

Drawing borderlines between science and religion is in itself very bad and very sinful. The sin is even deadlier when we realize that, in our Islamic school, several subjects are taught in a way contrary to our Islamic concepts and attitudes. They often conflict with our own principles.

We teach our boys and girls the Darwinian theory not as a scientific hypothesis, as it really is, nor as a mere scientific theory, which can be proved right or wrong. Giving it more scientific weight than it can really bear, we teach the theory in a documentary spirit as if it were a final, infallible, scientific fact.

The Darwinian theory, from its birth to the present day, has not achieved scientific absolutism. Neo-Darwinism, Julian Huxley being one of its most outstanding writers, confirms the uniqueness of man mentally, psychologically and even biologically. Huxley, a devout Darwinist and a steadfast atheist, has written a book entitled *Man in the Modern World*. He prefaces it with a lengthy chapter on 'The Uniqueness of Man', in which he says that the distance between man and ape is much larger than the distance between an ant or a cricket and the ape. But he goes on to say that modern science has placed man on a level not very different basically from that of the ant.

If that is the statement of a Darwinist atheist, should not we Muslims be over-cautious when we teach the Darwinian theory to our young generation in preparatory and secondary schools? Are we to ignore the fact that International Judaism, in order to exploit the Darwinian theory in its relentless campaign against religious beliefs, human values and higher principles, has propagated it and given it a considerable place in school curricula?

Anthropology, which is a direct outcome of Darwin's evolutionary theory and a continuation of it, is a foreign product, but our sons and daughters study anthropology in schools and universities. They are taught that the first man closely resembled the ape. He used to walk on hands and feet. When he stood on his feet to pluck fruit from the trees his figure straightened. His head, resting on his trunk, had the chance to grow in size. He then learnt to utter verbal sounds. His intelligence grew considerably and he was able to do many things.

Our students are also taught that the environment moulds man's life, his habits, traditions, feelings, thoughts and modes of behaviour.

The first statement is a direct echo of the Darwinian theory. No

52

scientific evidence to that effect is available. The second statement is a continuation of the same theory. It may apply to man in the absence of religious belief, it would be acceptable to an agnostic who claims that nothing is known of the existence of any God. A man without religious belief falls an easy prey to environment, that moulds his life, habits, traditions, feelings, thoughts and modes of behaviour. A single glance at the history of Islam will show us how this belief created a nation – a nation described by the Creator in this Quranic verse, 'Ye are the best of peoples, evolved for Mankind'; (Sura *Al-i-Imran*, verse 110), a nation now completely disconnected from its glorious past.

This does not mean that the environment has no control over man. Not at all. Islam spread and invaded many parts of the world. Wherever it was launched it absorbed the best that it could find in each environment and rendered them compatible with Islamic concepts, values and principles.

When we study modern anthropology we tend to refer to and copy Western anthropological thought and methods and completely ignore the impact of true and sound Islamic beliefs. We tacitly accept the suggestion which is contrary to, if not directly in conflict with the Islamic concept, that man is the child of his environment only and that man's history on earth is determined by the environment alone.

In our modern treatment of history we commit the same error. Man's history on earth is studied from two different points of view which are not only contrary but also contradictory to the Islamic concept. The first one regards the history of mankind as one of continued progression and growth, while the second measures human progress in terms of material and architectural advancement. Consequently, we admire and praise heathen civilizations such as the Pharaonic, Greek, Roman, Babylonian and Assyrian civilizations. The present civilization is also admired and considered the best and the most refined; very often much better and more refined than the generation of the Prophet's *Sahaba* (life Companions). If we do not actually say this we imply it by the way history is being taught.

From the Islamic point of view man has only two states of being regardless of his material progress. He is either 'in the best of moulds' or 'the lowest of the low': 'We have indeed created man in the best of moulds. Then do We debase him (to be) the lowest of the low. Except such as believe and do righteous deeds'. (Sura *Tin*, verses 4–6) Man is in the best of moulds when he believes in Allah and strictly follows His instructions; he is the lowest of the low when he does not believe in the

One and the Only God or follows instructions other than His. The material aspect of civilization, however great, is not the criterion of human progress. The Quran speaks of peoples who dominated the earth and founded great civilizations, but they were *jahiliyyin* (agnostics). They did not believe in the existence of God nor did they follow His divine instructions. They had their sciences which delighted them, but they did not derive much benefit from them. They did not follow the science Divine which aims at the good in this life and the hereafter. From the Islamic point of view ancient civilizations such as the Pharaonic, Greek, Roman Babylonian and Assyrian are considered *jahiliyyat* or agnostic. Islam also states that the generation of the Prophet's Companions was the best generation the earth has ever borne. Contemporary agnosticism with its avaricious, material civilization, gigantic scientific and technological progress is the worst that history has ever witnessed. The moral and spiritual downfall of man in this present age is such as has never occurred in history before.

The Islamic point of view refuses to circumscribe human history within its limited mundane duration, or to measure the achievements of mankind in relation to this period alone, saying that they are refined, progressive or reactionary. Secular and anti-secular achievements (they are inseparable) are taken into consideration when judgement is passed on a people. History is to be judged at both ends from its first to its very last. 'He hath created you; some are believers, and some are not'. Material civilization on earth is positively one of the criteria, for God created man for His particular purpose. 'It is He Who hath produced you from the earth and settled you therein.' (Sura *Hud*, verse 61) It is not the material achievements of man that count; they are but the foundations upon which his real achievements are built.

The true criterion of judgment is whether or not they are based on Divine commandments. Believers and non-believers alike can build a materialistic civilization on earth. But the believer uses it to bring him nearer to God, whereas the non-believer uses it to bring him closer to the devil. Our current studies ignore all this. History is taught in the way European agnostics teach it. They are the authorities to whom we often resort and refer.

In sociology we teach our students the theories of Durkhiem, the Jew, which conflict with the Islamic view. Durkhiem cancels all the stable values in human life. He says that religion, morals, marriage, the family as a social unit are not innate. They are the workings of the group mind which confirms or rejects them as it pleases.

54

In psychology we teach Freud's theories on sex as well as other theories which refuse to recognize religion as an indivisible part of human nature. These theories do not regard religion as a basis for evaluating human nature.

Physical sciences such as chemistry, physics, biology, astrology, mathematics, engineering, medicine etc. are isolated from divine knowledge. We make a more serious mistake when we teach our children that Nature has created the universe and directs and governs it and that physical laws are arbitrary, absolute and inevitable.

Nature is a pagan word used in Europe in place of the word God. A capital 'N' emphasizes its ideological significance and the great esteem in which it is held. Europeans have had so many problems, spiritual as well as moral, with their church that they were made to give up their ecclesiastical God in whose name the church enslaved and oppressed them. They invented a churchless god, with no commitments, and called it Nature. To this man-made god they attributed the creation, direction and administration of the universe. As Darwin says, 'Nature creates everything, and there is no limit to its creativity'.

How do we Muslims allow this pagan and agnostic word 'Nature' to run smoothly on our tongues? We go even further and have it written in books which we prescribe for our pupils. When we teach the Darwinian theory in this manner, and deal with history, geography, sociology, psychology, education, economics, physical science in a non-Islamic spirit and from a non-Islamic point of view, how can we produce a Muslim generation of school children and university students?

This, of course, cannot be achieved since in every curriculum we teach, and in every lesson we give there is a great deal of anti-Islamic propaganda involved. What is the value of a formal self-centred lesson on religion if it is given in the midst of an anti-spiritual, non-religious atmosphere? What is the significance of such a lesson in this tumultuous multitude of non-Islamic currents, undercurrents and cross-currents? The lesson itself has shrunk to the proportions of small textual pieces to be memorized and tested at the end of the year. The situation is grave indeed. Striking and immediate reforms are called for in our system of education; reforms that should shake the very foundation of the whole system.

If we are serious about giving religion its true place in educational curricula we have to do two things almost simultaneously. First, we must not restrict religious guidance to the formal traditional lesson on religion. Second, we must reconsider the syllabuses devised for this particular lesson and re-evaluate them in most parts of the Muslim world.

The object of religious education (Islamic education in particular) is to produce a Muslim man or woman. This end cannot be achieved through a few disintegrated pieces of religious information to be learnt by heart and tested at the end of the school year, especially if one's concepts, attitudes, morals and modes of behaviour are all non- or anti-Islamic.

If we do not at present possess all the necessary tools of Islamic education, if we don't apply the Divine law in our actual life and if we don't make it imperative that the home and the street should uphold and enforce Islamic teachings and morals, nothing then remains to be done except to exploit the potentialities of the educational curriculum in an attempt to fill the wide gap in our lives or at least part of it. This can be done if we revise all our curricula and methodology and rebuild them on a sound Islamic basis. Then we shall have in our possession more than one curriculum and more than one lesson for Islamic education in addition to the formal one. Islamic education should in fact be in operation right from the very beginning of the school day to the very end, and from the first year of primary education up to the last of university education.

This does not mean that all our lessons should be transformed into sermons. Far from it. For this will not lead us to the desired end, nor will it create the desired effect.

The Prophet (Peace be on him), the most beloved person to his followers throughout the entire history of mankind, delivered religious sermons to his companions only now and then as occasion demanded lest, as the books of *Sira* (the Prophet's biography) relate, they get tired or disinterested. Would life be worth living if we, ordinary human beings that we are, turn it into a series of everlasting sermons? A religious sermon, unavoidable, should not last more than a few minutes out of the whole day. Other curricula and lessons will contribute to the creation and growth of the religious consciousness desired in a way completely different from that of sermonizing.

Take a biology lesson for instance. If we cross out the word 'Nature' from our textbooks and replace it by the proper word 'Allah' (the Almighty), what will the result be? We will live in His divine presence during the whole lesson with a consciousness hypersensitive to His miraculous creativity. Is there any single lesson in biology which does not draw our consciousness to God's creativity when taught in the proper scientific manner that attributes the act of creation to the true sole Creator? What part of the living organism does not stir consciousness? Who makes the seed sprout forth from the earth? Who pushes the stem upwards, contrary to the earth's gravitational pull? Who makes the flower blossom and bear fruit? Who gives it colour, taste and smell? Can there be another god besides God?

There are so many who's and so many what's; thousands of questions and tens of thousands of more questions about such miraculous creativity. It is God and God alone who has performed those miracles.

Take a physics or a chemistry lesson for example. Who has given matter its specific properties? Who has made bodies expand when heated and increase in size when it freezes? Who has made flat the surface of all liquids, except that of mercury, which is convex? Who has made a particular element chemically interact with another particular element and not with any other? Who has made water of two elements – hydrogen and oxygen, both inflammable – and which, when compounded, may extinguish flaming fires? Can there be another god besides God?

Take a geophysics lesson for instance; the earth's crust and climate: mountains, valleys, seas, rivers, clouds, rains, winds . . . etc.

Take this lesson when taught in the light of its inherent scientific truth and not shrouded in modern agnosticism which does not allow the name of God to be mentioned in any scientific research in order to maintain its 'purity' by not introducing a supernatural element into it. How is it that modern agnosticism is blind to the fact that Nature, to which creativity is attributed, is in this sense harmful to scientific research? What, specifically, is Nature after all? How and when did it assume its infinite creativity? Do we deceive ourselves, as contemporary European agnostics want us to, into absolute belief in the creativity of Nature and forget that, being the sole creator, it is a supernatural element whose 'being' is ambiguous, vague and unknowable? Is not giving things false names contrary to the true scientific spirit?

Take a lesson in astronomy. How many spiritual journeys we can make into God's miraculous phenomena in this universe which is, simultaneously, miraculously huge and orderly? Our minds as well as our finest and most developed machinery fail to reach the heights of its vastness, or conceive the hugeness of its stars and planets, or comprehend the miraculous precision in their undisturbed circulation. 'It is not permitted to the Sun to catch up with the Moon, nor can the Night

57

outstrip the Day: Each (just) swims along in (its own) orbit (according to Law)'. (Sura *Ya-sin*, verse 40).

These lessons, spontaneous and without the least unnatural pretention, will give us a chance to revive religious consciousness in the hearts of the learners. When taught properly, they will make our hearts feel the greatness of God and consequently fear and love him most. This is the Quranic method of exposing God's phenomena before the eyes of His creation. 'Soon will We show them Our Signs in the (furthest) regions (of the earth), and in their souls, until it becomes manifest to them that this is the Truth.' (Sura *Fussilat*, verse 53).

Contemporary European agnostics refuse to adopt and apply this method simply because they are engaged in a constant and absurd war with God. They regard God as their most hated and feared enemy. Look at Julian Huxley, to whom we previously referred, when he speaks of the contemporary Prometheus. He says that man, now fully equipped with knowledge and sole master of his environment, must of necessity assume the power which, in times of ignorance and helplessness, he attributed to God, and become himself God. God forgives us this blind heresy!

We address our Westernized intellectuals who, like the Europeans, refuse to mention the word God in any scientific research lest human minds lose sight of the law of causality which moves, orders and controls the universe, and become metaphysical minds. We tell them that Islamic education does not make people lose sight of the law of causality and its intricate connections; it refers it, after studying it thoroughly, to its originator, to Allah (Praise be to Him). The more we learn about the creativity of Allah, the closer our hearts will be brought to Him. Thus the word of God: 'Those truly fear God, among His Servants, who have knowledge'. (Sura *Fatir*, verse 28).

When we have finished with these lessons which give us a good chance to create and develop religious consciousness, we shall move on to some other types of lessons which play another role in Islamic education. This role involves putting human ideology in Islamic moulds, *i.e.* looking into the innermost nature of every single physical phenomenon with a purely Islamic eye. History, human geography, education, psychology, sociology, economics . . . etc. will have this end in view.

A history lesson, in fact, is a lesson in education. It is really so whether we know it or not, whether we intend it to be or not. The methodology we apply when we teach history makes its own impressions on the learner. Any attempt at segregating a history lesson from the impressions it leaves on the learner is impossible. If the impressions are sound and healthy they will create a proper insight. On the contrary, if they are wrong and unhealthy they will create a harmful and dismal effect on our souls.

We have made a brief reference to the Islamic methodology adopted in history teaching. We cannot possibly avoid, when we apply any methodology whatsoever to our teaching of history, searching for an answer to a specific question, an answer which will provide us with criteria in the light of which we can evaluate men and events. The basic question is: What is the end of human existence on this earth? Without having a sufficiently clear answer to this question history turns out to be a mere relation of events and narratives. This is not history at all. Interpretation of historical events, after examining the facts and investigating the dates, is the real work of the historian. On what basis is he to interpret, and by what criterion is he to measure?

Western historiography, born in an agnostic irreligious atmosphere, is based on the idea that the ultimate end of human existence on this earth is to erect materialistic civilization and enjoy the best that the earth can offer. On this basis, countries and nations, individuals and communities are assessed. Western historiography preoccupies itself with recording and assessing material strength, military supremacy, political authority, facilitating life and enjoying its pleasures, amongst which are a handful of immaterial values such as thought, art, moral, social and human values which occupy a tiny corner in history and not its unique basic field.

The method adopted in Islamic historiology, born in an atmosphere of Islamic belief, is altogether different though it does not overlook anything other historiologies mention and cherish. That the goal of human existence on earth is God's worship is the core and substance of Islamic historiology. 'I have created the jinn and men only that they may worship Me.' (Sura *Al-Dhariyat*, verse 56). 'Say: "My prayers, my sacrifice, my life and my death, are all for Allah, the Lord of the Worlds. He has no peer".' (Sura *Al-Anam*, verses 162–3).

Westernized intellectuals may imagine, at the very outset, that this viewpoint is too narrow, limited and restricted. The concept of divine worship, among later Muslim generations, grew narrower and narrower until it became at last confined to mere rituals. Such is not the concept of worship in Islam. It simply comprises *everything* in man's life: his belief, work, thought, feeling and conduct. The verse in the Sura

Al-Anam explicitly emphasises that: 'Say: "My prayers, sacrifice, *my life and my death*, are all for Allah, the Lord of the Worlds".' Man's entire life, even death itself, is for Allah, the Lord of the Worlds, the Peerless. The Islamic concept of divine worship encompasses all that man does, thinks and feels only on one condition that he, body and soul, mind and heart, should commit himself wholly to God and God's orders. Hence Islamic historiological methodology does not neglect anything contained in other types of methodology. It records and counts everything. Not a single event escapes attention. Islam assesses everything and weighs it by the divine scale. Has every thought, feeling or action been devoted to the worship of Allah, the end of human existence on this earth? 'Many were the Ways of Life that have passed away before you: travel through the earth, and see what was the end of those who rejected Truth.' (Sura, *al-Imran* verse 137).

What would the consequences in the hereafter be as God has told us?

Facts will remain unchanged in the Islamic historiological methodology and other types of methodologies. Not a single historical reality will be neglected. When the Pharaohs are mentioned nothing in the gigantic civilization they founded will be overlooked or underestimated: their statues, pyramids, temples, cities, construction projects, military expeditions, tools of civilization, arts, sciences. When we mention the Greeks none of their philosophies and their sciences will be ignored or undervalued. When we mention the Romans we shall have to consider and record all that they built: architecture, discipline and organization. All this will be evaluated, as mentioned, by God's criteria. Did they live their lives and die their deaths in the cause of Allah, the Lord of the Worlds, the Peerless? Or did they live and die for some other cause which does not realize the real end of human existence? In other words, were they believers, in the Islamic sense of the word, or were they agnostics? If it is decided that those nations did prove to be agnostic, this will then be their real significance in the eyes of proper history.

When a student becomes accustomed to looking into the nature of the individual physical phenomenon with a purely Islamic insight when studying history, sociology, economics, education, psychology, literature, the arts, his thinking power will be harnessed to Islamic controls, and his ideology will be cast in the Islamic mould. Besides, the first lessons previously referred to will create and enhance religious consciousness, making the human heart live in the presence of Allah, to fear and love Him. 'They hope for His Mercy and fear His Wrath.'

(Sura *Al-Isra'a*, verse 57). Any type of education which does not preach religious sermons or encourage 'sermonizing', in the familiar sense of the word, is a purely scientific one. Only divine science can bring the consciousness of the servant closer to his Lord's, as long as the servant grows more conscious of the things around him. 'Say, "Oh my Lord! advance me in knowledge".' (Sura *Ta Ha*, verse 114).

There is not sufficient scope here to elaborate the Islamic viewpoint as regards the subjects aforementioned, particularly sociology, psychology, education, literature and art. This should be attempted in detailed and lengthy studies.

Western Capitalist democracies approach these subjects from a capitalist democratic point of view. Communist and Socialist countries approach the same subjects from a communist and socialist viewpoint. It is a pity that our Muslim schools and universities do not study these subjects from a purely Islamic viewpoint. Some people may consider it a queer idea to accommodate in our minds, a flimsy whim or even a prejudice unbecoming of the true spirit of scientific investigation. Some being completely ignorant of their religion, may go so far as to ask: Is there an Islamic point of view applicable to such subjects? Isn't science, strictly speaking, a science that is not and should not be related to religion?

Definitely and most decisively No! We can achieve a lot in the field of Islamic education if we steer our curricula and methodologies into creating and enhancing religious consciousness on the one hand and harnessing our ideology to the Islamic viewpoint on the other. If Crusade imperialism had, in most of our Muslim countries, hidden the Islamic point of view from our school curricula it is now high time for us, especially at this conference, to go back to ourselves and know our spiritual entity.

Assuming that all this is done in our schools and our methodology employed in the manner previously mentioned, there remains only the formal lesson on religion. When all other lessons combined play their significant role in education, no objection will be raised to the existence of a formal lesson entirely devoted to giving information bearing directly on religion every individual Muslim ought to know. Such information will cover belief, jurisprudence, recitation of the Holy Quran, Hadith (the Prophet's Sayings) and all other items which, apparently non-existent in other lessons, constitute a self-contained specialization. There is no harm at all in quoting the Holy Quran or the Hadith when we deal with any scientific lesson or the scientific theory aforementioned provided that we have this end in view, i.e. to reinforce, substantiate and reinterpret all scientific data phenomena in terms of Islamic data.

A lesson entirely devoted to religion is urgently needed to convey all necessary information about the duties of worship, dealings and judgements. But why do we insist on making it so rigid, so lifeless, so insipid, so far from the attractive tolerance of Islam and its illuminating spirit?

If we preach that a biology, a physics, a chemistry or an astronomy lesson should be exploited to create and intensify religious consciousness, wouldn't a specialized religious lesson be more entitled to do that? Why do we cram the formal religious lesson with rigid texts and purely mental controversies which, in no sense, serve the doctrine or bring the heart one inch closer to God? Why should we not follow the lines of the Quran which was revealed to instruct the people in their belief, law, duties or worship and dealings?

The Holy Quran guides religious consciousness through a labyrinth of mental controversies whether the subject of those controversies be divinity, the hereafter, the Prophet's narration, morals, juridical judgements or the fight for Allah. There are no Quranic verses involving jurisprudence which do not remind us of Allah to make the human heart look up to Him in submissive awe. Why shouldn't we be Quranists when we draw up our religious curricula?

The ages which have elapsed which made Muslims of a certain period transform religion into an endless series of complicated philosophical and metaphysical controversies, were not the most flourishing of Islamic ages. It was a foreign intrusive contagion which overpowered Muslims, during a particular period, spoiling the purity of Islamic ideology, and distorting its simple truths, clarity of vision and vitality.

We lose little in fact if we pass over those ages and resort unhesitatingly to the true, unambiguous and rich resources of Islam and its sound and real examples: to the Holy Book and the Sunna (the Prophet's Sayings and Doings), to the Prophet's life stories and the life stories of his Companions and followers, and particularly, to the existing Quranic method of dealing with all controversies included in this religion.

There is no scope here for more details, for this paper was originally intended to give mere glimpses to light up the way to the right path. May Allah Help us and Guide us to the Right Path, Amen!

Translated from Arabic by
Muhammad Abdul Majeed Barghout

Chapter Three

Education in an Ideological State

A. K. Brohi

Allahbakhsh Khudabakhsh Brohi, an eminent Advocate by profession, a philosopher by intellectual discipline and a mystic in spiritual attachment, held important ministerial posts in the Pakistan Cabinet, was the architect of the first Constitution of Pakistan and is at present the Law Minister of Pakistan. Besides his monumental work on the Constitution of Pakistan, he has to his credit such other books as: *Adventures in Self-Expression*; *Fundamental Law of Pakistan*; *Islam and the Modern World*.

Pakistan is an ideological state. And by that, at its irreducible minimum, is meant a state which is founded on a manner of thinking or an idea characteristic of the people belonging to it. Our constitution declares that Islam shall be the State religion of Pakistan. It is also pledged to eradicate exploitation in all forms in order that the gradual fulfilment of fundamental principle 'from each according to his ability to each according to his work' should be realized. It would thus appear that all operations of our state, in the last resort, are inspired by an ideology that lies at the root of our people's commitment to lead the sort of life which is sanctioned by Islam – with particular emphasis upon the need to realize an egalitarian society.

By education we understand a *participation* in a cultural process by which successive generations of men and women take their place in our national history upon the foundation of an ideological commitment to the Islamic way of life, and a certain manner of thinking and action conforming to its tenets and commands.

By sheer circumstance of his birth man is endowed with a certain plasticity which enables him, thanks to this cultural process, to *inherit* the fruit of labour that has been put forward by the human race just to be able *to learn how to tackle the tasks of life* – in short, to have access to the civilization of the past. He also learns not only to participate in the enterprise of history but is also enabled *to make an effective* contribution towards the furthering and advancing of the cause of mankind. 'The essential Nature of Civilization', says Albert Schweitzer, 'does not lie in its material achievements, but in the fact that individuals keep in mind the ideals of the perfecting of man and the improvement of the social and political conditions of the peoples and of mankind as a whole and that their habit of thought is determined in living and constant fashion by such ideals. Only when individuals work in this way, as spiritual forces, and are brought to bear upon themselves and on Society, is the possibility given of solving problems which have been produced by the facts of life and of attaining to a general progress which is valuable in every respect.'

The human child is born helpless, unlike the young ones of other animal species, and the educational process which commences with its infancy is co-terminus with the total range of life itself. It should be the aim of the educational process to familiarize the young child with the products of mental evolution of the human race so as to bring him up-to-date and also to give him those *inner resources with which to appreciate and enjoy life* and to make a worthwhile contribution towards the all-important tasks of bringing relief and redemption to the total life of mankind as a whole.

In the perspective of Islam, the functional value of life necessarily takes on a dual character: Life in this world is regarded as possessing, over and above its conventional role, yet another *viz. if it is properly lived it is capable of becoming the seed-plot of the Hereafter*. In a secular perspective, life has no trans-historic reference; temporal existence is all there is to it – in other words, it becomes co-extensive with history. But in a religious perspective such as that of Islam, it becomes a means of self-transcendence – in the sense that going beyond the frontiers of history it aspires to have a glimpse of the Eternal Here beyond. An individual who believes in such a life necessarily so conducts the operations of his life here below as to win of the reward of that life 'which is *better* and *eternal*' (*Khairun wa Abqā*).

As any one can see, it makes all the difference in the world whether life is lived in a secular setting or in a larger context furnished by the religious perspective.

The religion of Islam takes care to see that man lives a successful life here below but then, since for it, *this* life is a prelude to real life to come, it sets limits to certain instinctive cravings of the lower self of man in order to enable him to undergo the process of preparation which is required if one is to be admitted to the precincts of the higher life. It is in this sense that this world was regarded as a 'Valley of Soul Making' by John Keats, the famous English poet. For man, according to Shakespeare 'being ripe' here below was all. In his immortal lines, we have it:

64

Men must adore their going hence
As even their coming hither
– for *ripeness is all*.

Islam too admonishes us to be vicegerents of God on Earth – we are invited thus to improve the world and by constant remembrance of the Lord to offer to God's light a transparent medium.

Religious belief, by and large, is a sort of unavoidable response that finite life, knowing its earthly limitations and boundaries within which it operates, makes to the Infinite life – which it views as some kind of Higher Presence. The choice before man is, so it seems to me, not between having belief and no belief but between *right belief and wrong belief*. We have to believe, by which is meant that we have to adopt an attitude to our total environment – although, all we are in contact with, both in space and time, is only a partial environment, being a mere segment of the total environment that our faculties are able to establish contact with. Our belief therefore takes us beyond the evidence which is available to us and gives us a view of the total environment. This is what is attributable to the primacy of prophetic consciousness precisely in the sense that but for the Prophets of Universal Religion who have been inspired by God to inform us about our real position in the Scheme of Things, man would have been without any sure foundation of belief upon which to conduct the operations of his life.

Care should be taken to remember that although there are many religions in the historical sense, religions that are of high and low degree, there is also, what may be called, for want of a better expression, 'Religion-in-general' which is a concomitant of, and just springs from the human situation itself. If all the common forms of religious beliefs known to us were by some design abolished, there would still remain a need for mankind to have some religious attitude to live by and some form of religion would necessarily emerge to take the place of all the religious systems that had been thus abolished.

Thus defined, in its most general universal sense, a recent American philosopher puts the essence of religious belief as follows:

'Religion as a man's deepest solicitude, is the concern he shows for the fate of that which he accounts most valuable. However primitive or advanced their outlook, men will always prize something above all other things; will recognize environing forces on which their fortunes ultimately depend; and will put this prize and this recognition together in a more or less *hopeful belief*'.

To the extent to which this working definition of religion is relevant, it could be said that a believer in the mission of the last Prophet would prize above everything else the sanctity of his relationship with his Maker and thereby become cognizant of his accountability to Him for conforming to the Divine mandate which is what Islam is really about. This Divine law takes for man, the form of the will of his Maker, and man's *obedience* to it is designed to enable him to register progress in the direction of reaching higher vistas of human excellence. What is more, such is the Nature of Divine Law, that he can neglect the injunctions and mandates of his religious creed only at the risk of suffering a serious setback on his way to the goal that counts – which is none other than that of his having vision of God. Islam helps its votaries both in the matter of coping with the challenges of life here below as also for obtaining a reward of Eternal Life in the hereafter. Thus the essence of Islam lies in a religious belief which no man really can do without, if only because its adoption spares him the ravages of doubt and saves him from its Hamlet-like paralysis of human will. Such a belief imparts to his life a certain consistency and momentum and gives to him the moral and intellectual resources, a sort of spiritual stamina, with which to confront and combat all the difficulties that beset the course of his life here below and to be admitted to the company of the Elect in the life to come.

During the last 200 years or so, the foundation of this religious belief in the essential sense we have propounded, has been questioned and to a considerable extent undermined. Today we are really living in God-less times, in this bleak and barren age of ours. Man does not acknowledge the Higher Presence any more. He considers that he is the master of all he surveys.

For undermining man's faith in a Presence higher than his own, the device adopted has been to show that the origin of man's religious consciousness is to be traced to *his sense of fear* and gods and goddesses in whom he believed in ancient times have been exhibited as representing some sort of his own inventions – agents that more or less had provided for him a sense of security against that fear. Now that science and scientific knowledge have come to the rescue of man, it is being argued, with a show of finality, that man has the capacity to control his environment and so become master of his fate. As he is no longer a slave of his circumstances, it is being argued that he does not any more need religious belief in the ancient gods in whom his forefathers believed. By thus explaining the origin of religious belief, which after all was no more than an aspect of man's primitive consciousness, man's essential craving to rehabilitate his relationship with the world around him is denounced as being no better than an expression of his infantile wish to find security in a world which is no longer hostile to him. All this is being done in the name of science and that too by resorting to the simple device of substituting the history of an institution for the logic of its present day operation. But the scientist somehow forgets that the moment the *One True God* is displaced in the life of men, numerous false gods step in to fill in the void – whether these be called 'the State', 'the Worship of Humanity', 'Gospel of dialectical materialism or of economic force' or any other description of that type does not really matter. No man in fact is able to do without God – his choice is only between worshipping the One true God and some false ones.

Thus the critics of *communism* for instance have been able to show *that communism itself is a religion* in that it has its *paradise* called the *class-less society*; it has its temple of worship, called the *dialectical materialism*; it has even its ritual sacrifices, the *liquidation pogroms of the enemies of communism* that somehow go about undetected for quite some time before the swift and sudden realization that somehow dawns upon the powers that be that by means of organized measures they be done away with.

Whether one says that communism is 'atheistic' or that it has made 'a god of economic force' ultimately depends on whether one is thinking in terms of that *particular religious belief* or in terms of *religion in general*. Similar remarks apply to cults which judged by conventional standards can be described as atheistic. That is how, for instance, the fundamental teaching of Buddhism is interpreted by some scholars – since it too recognizes no God in the conventional sense. But then, in so far as it teaches that Nirvana is the supreme good and that by following the *law*, one is able to reach the supreme good, to that extent at any rate, Buddhism too would appear to be a religion *par excellence if only because it enables man to transcend the claims of his biological being and 'to prize something within himself beyond everything else'*. Buddhism upholds the claims of Higher Life by teaching its votaries to reach the State of Nirvana – a state where the mere animal cravings and low desires cease to menace his earthly existence.

The fostering of a sound religious belief I submit is the main task of Education. Unfortunately education in our times is often described as being either *religious or non-*religious (or *secular*) – that is to say education that teaches the elements of theology, religious law etc. and education that teaches how to qualify for liberal callings like that of the law, medicine or engineering etc. These are supposed to be *two different kinds of education*. In the last category comes education in sciences and in arts which are taught in our schools, in our colleges and in our universities. But I, for one, do not see how education can at all be so artificially divided; all education is an attempt to *cultivate the soil of an individual's life*, to kindle the Divine Spark that is lying buried in all of us. If education does minister to that sacred flame and makes it glow with light, well and good, but if it does not, in my reckoning it does not merit the name of education, no matter what else it is able to do. If there be one thing in man which he ought to prize above everything else or, to put it concretely, if there is one thing needed to make us worthy of our high station as human beings, that Destiny which has been assigned to us, then it should be the aim of education to enable us to acquire it. The human Mind is impressionable at all ages and it is the task of education to see that it remains impressionable right to the end of our days. Education is thus education for life. It enables the best in us to be brought forth, to be nurtured and its cause advanced. It imparts to us the awareness of our real place in the scheme of things. The extent to which we have learnt to discipline ourselves in the historical present in order that our dormant faculties may flower and qualify us for the reward of a higher life is precisely the extent to which we are educated.

It is true that there is a certain type of education which prepares us to tackle what may be called the practical tasks of life; here the aim is to teach certain technical skills in order that we may enable the students to gainfully employ themselves for the purposes of earning their livelihood. But I contend, in this context, that even this sort of discipline, if it is not geared to the basic purpose of highlighting the best of which we, as human beings, are capable, is anyhow not worth much and hardly deserves being regarded as the final consummation of the educational process. Similar remarks apply to the artificial distinctions that are often drawn between education being *personal* and *social* or between *self-education* and education acquired by *external agencies*, or between the education of the *mind* and education of the *body* or between the *education of the intellect* and the *education of emotions and the wills* and so on and so forth. All these artificial partition walls that are often erected to set forth the terrains of various types of education hardly do justice to the over-all purpose of education. The whole of the educational process which is, as remarked above, as large as life itself and traverses the whole *gamut* of human civilization and culture has for its aim the development of individual and of Society of which he is the member.

68

Similarly the distinction between professional education and education in the humanities or what is also called general education, although useful to pin-point the specific goals they are designed to reach – the former helping the student to qualify for handling some profession and the latter to secure his development as a human being – but all these are equally artificial distinctions in the sense that the over-all and real meaning of education is thereby blurred.

There are certain truisms about education, regarded as a cultural process, which it is necessary to recall in this context in order to make intelligible the points that are sought to be made in this paper. First of these is that we must educate our students in such a manner that *they acquire the capacity to educate themselves for the rest of their lives*. Education in this sense must teach men and women how to teach themselves; how to learn from even the resources which are not obviously designed directly to advance the educational purposes. In the second place, to be educated may be easy enough (given the encounter between a mind that has a certain degree of the power of uptake and a teacher who has the capacity to mould the lives of his students), but a far more difficult thing to attain is for *those who are educated to stay educated and not to slide back to an animal state in an atavistic style*.

The curriculum of studies which is often divided into 'arts' and 'sciences' and these in their turn into various sub-branches, to say nothing of subjects such as history, philosophy, literature etc. serves a useful purpose in that it enables the students to specialize in a particular sphere of knowledge. But then an attempt should also be made to fix the student's attention on that 'All-inclusive-togetherness of things which is both the first step of naiveté and the last step of sophistication'. Its object is that dimly outlined and exhaustible immensity which is called 'the universe' or 'the world'. Here we are reminded of the wise saying of a Roman Philosopher who had remarked, 'Since I am human, there is nothing human which is outside the range of my concern and study.'

We must enable our students not only to be well informed in the sense that they are made aware of the inheritance which has been bequeathed to them by the human race, but they themselves have to be drilled into becoming serviceable agents that will impart a new direction or creative impulse to history. And this they can do if they are helped to form correct judgements in relation to the data that has been submitted for their consideration. It is no use acquiring an encyclopedic mind if that mind at the same time is so stunted in its growth that it cannot form a correct judgement as to even elementary matters.

Since I deny that in an ideological state such as ours which is constitutionally declared to be founded upon religious principles, there is any valid distinction between religious and non-religious education, I ought to explain the basic reason that compels me to say so. This has reference to the strategy of the religion of Islam itself. The religion of Islam is not just one religion amongst others, as if it were launched in history in competition with other religions. Islam says all religion is one – the total religious process which has been at work since the dawn of human consciousness right up to its maturity is affirmed by Islam. All it has said is that the *crowning* summit of that process reached its final expression in the Holy Writ, that is, the Quran. Islam, rightly understood, does away with the claim that there have been many religions. The religion with God, says the Quran, is Islam. From Adam down, all the Prophets of the Universal Religion were Muslims and they taught Islam. Of course, in the earlier phase of its development the teachings of the Universal religion had to reckon with the immature mind of man but as man began to mature, the guardians that he had one time needed were no longer necessary – since, as a mature mind, he can be trusted to apply his independent power of reason to see what is at stake and to apply correctly principles of universal religion for the solution of problems that beset his way. In the framework of all other historical religions, the distinction between education being religious and non-religious obtains, if only because these religions have had a narrower scope when it came to the regulation of human life. But Islam in its final form, as preached by Prophet Muhammad (on whom be peace) rules life in its totality and is therefore ubiquitous in its range and scope. That is why with the advent of the last prophetic message the distinction between religious and non-religious education has really disappeared. All that the believers do here below is conditioned by the attitude that Islam fosters with the result that whatever we do in His Holy Name and for His sake, becomes a religious act. Everything therefore depends on *niyyat* or *intention* and the reason why we do things. The distinction between acts being religious and non- or irreligious does not lie in the acts themselves but in the inwardness of human disposition to act, for it is precisely at this point that man reflects his obedience to the higher law in freedom. That is why there is no compulsion in Religion. Man must now freely surrender at the altar of Divine Will. On the external plane no distinction between religious and non-religious act as discernible. Indeed this distinction is traceable only to the inner dimension in the being of man – it is there that man in all his humility enters into communion with his Lord and Master. In this communion, man reaches his highest station that it is possible in principle to attain.

So very true in this approach that according to Dr. Robert Briffault 'The old discredited notions of medieval Christianity that the supremely important act about the man was what he believed, that according as that belief, that creed, that opinion was true or false, he himself was to be counted good or bad, that his moral worth, his conduct were but the outward reflection of his intellectual attitude, *that notion that has come to be branded as infamous and abhorrent was, as a matter of fact, strictly and incontrovertibly correct*. Only the incongruity, and inconsistency of the historical situation which brought about the advocacy and special pleadings of Locke, Bayle, Voltaire for the toleration of the rationality of thought and reduced the values and foundations of validity, legitimacy or illegitimacy, right or wrong thereby giving rise to that outrageous and intolerable modern tolerance which regards every opinion as equally respectable, could divest intellectual belief of moral value or significance.'

The Central institution in the life of Islam is the Mosque. From the days of Prophet and for quite a few centuries thereafter it was a place not only for saying prayers, but also for taking political decisions, as also for receiving deputations of persons who would visit the *Amīru'l-Mu'minīn* on official business. It was also a place for rendering judicial decisions to resolve conflicts between individuals.

The Mosque has this sanctity especially in view of the fact that it is a place set apart for worship although, in the Muslim perspective, the whole earth is to be treated as a mosque if only because one can pray anywhere one likes – since according to Islam, God is everywhere and no formal altar is required for saying one's prayers. A Muslim's home was *supposed to be an extension of the mosque* and was to be regarded with as much sanctity. There is in Islam no distinction between things being sacred or profane. The impurity if at all is in the heart of man, and that is why he had to be purified by subjecting him to the rituals of religious processes. Indeed, one of the main tasks of the Prophet was to *purify his people* and to *teach them their destiny* and *to make them wise*.

Now surely this programme of (a) purifying the individual, (b) of helping him to regard the world as the sanctuary of the spirit and (c) to give him the inner disposition to keep himself constantly available in the service of Lord, requires that man ought to be educated to be able successfully to undertake these tasks. Whatever helps us to impart this to the younger generation of students would be education in the real sense of that term and without this much education, the ideological state as seen in the framework of Islamic values is not a possibility. It hardly requires being said that these things no one learns in the womb of his mother. Indeed, all of us have to be taught these things by our parents at home and later on in the mosque – our schools and colleges ought to be the extension of the Mosque. No education, as seen from this wider perspective, can claim supremacy unless it aspires to do what the Prophet of Islam did for the human race – he came to take man out from *the darkness to light whereas the counter-initiatory forces of his time were taking man from light to darkness.*

Since the Prophet of Islam is the Last Prophet to bring the revealed word of God and after him no other Prophet would come, man has in consequence really become master in his own house. He cannot any more afford to await the advent of some *Messiah* to show him the way. The way has already been shown and, what is more, the way that has been shown is in the nature of a *straight path* which by itself takes the traveller to the goal. And furthermore there is the light of God perennially showing the way to any individual who means to negotiate it. Consequently, for the believer, the task of reaching the goal is not as difficult as it used to be at one time. But this also argues for the priority of the educational process. No wonder the Quran begins with the word *iqra'* – to read.

There is an aspect of the problem of national education to which I would like to advert in order to avoid some possible misunderstandings, which may otherwise be occasioned in view of some of the observations I have made touching and concerning the role of national education in an ideological state. As is well known, whenever education is explicitly directed to a definite and pre-conceived end, it is exposed by its critics to the *charge of indoctrination* i.e. it becomes inimical to what is called free society, in that it fosters rigidity, fanaticism and closed-mindedness. This is the contention of Karl Popper in his famous book *'Open Society and its Enemies'*. From ancient times the case of Spartan education is often cited in support of this view. Education in Sparta had been geared to the pursuit of military purpose and of course to that extent it was pre-eminently successful. This is also said about the Jesuit education in the 16th century – in that it too was successful in producing 'a specific blend of scholasticism, Latin humanism and Catholic orthodoxy which proved to be too old a bottle to contain the new wines of scientific thought, vernacular literature and secular thought'. In our

72

own time we have the extreme examples of education being conducted by Nazis and Communists in a doctrinaire fashion. In some sense it is only too true to say that the education which has an expressed bias in favour of an ideology, is *successful* in producing a certain type of individual but at the same time it also narrows his mind and virtually forecloses the possibility of that much degree of openness of mind which one has to have in order to be receptive to truth in all its forms and manifestations. Nazism, for instance, produced in the German youth a passion for racial superiority of the Aryan race, virtues of military discipline, of unquestioning obedience to the Führer and practically everything else was made subservient to this master passion of devotion to the great dictator. This is true of communist societies also. Out of this predicament arises the fundamental dilemma of education which may, in the word of R. B. Perry, be stated thus: 'To define in advance an end result and then to seek, by all possible means, to achieve it, is held to be too narrow and too repressive, too authoritarian. But if, on the other hand, there is no end in view, educational activity is confused and incoherent. Its various parts and successive phases do not add up to anything. Without a definition of the end there is no test by which means can be selected, and no standard by which practice can be criticized and improved.'

This charge, however, cannot be urged in case education is made subservient to the principles which are sanctioned by Islam if only because Islam merely gives us a bold outline of the kind of 'Supreme Doctrine' upon which it would like to rest our view of life and of the world and leaves out a great deal to be dealt with by our own creativity and inventiveness. It is as if a legislature passed a law of a general nature to achieve a well-defined objective and handed over the ways and means of realizing that purpose to be achieved by means of Rules of Bye-laws which the government of the day is empowered to make. There is, in such a case, a great deal of authority delegated to the government. This is also the case with Islam: commitment to the ideology of Islam virtually leaves the man free so long as he is loyal to the overall purpose of securing the moral and material progress of society within the limits of Divine Law. General guide-lines along which this development is to take place are stated in the Holy Book and suggested in the Practice of the Prophet. There is no such thing as a narrow, rigid and authoritarian basis for a programme of national education that can be found within the framework of Islamic ideology. Islam is all out for open enquiry and demands loyalty to facts. Islam enjoins observation of facts of nature, and of mind and history and recommends its votaries to reflect upon signs in Nature, in our inner self and history. Indeed Islam came to protest against authority, rigidity and narrowness of pre-existing religious doctrines that had somehow been petrified if not mutilated by priestly interpretation of the Divine Law. And this is made clear by our reading of early Islamic literature. The early Islamic scholars travelled the length and breadth of the world, translated the great classics that were available in foreign languages and re-stated the pre-existing religious doctrines by which various civilizations and cultures of the pre-Islamic phase of Human History were influenced. This catholocity of taste on their part arose from the fact that Islam itself avowedly being a *religion of affirmation* was never viewed by them as being something antagonistic to pre-existing faiths and cultures. Islam, thus it would appear, had come to rescue mankind from the narrowness and the authoritarian bigotry of the dark ages of Europe. A commitment to the ideology of Islam therefore can never in its turn foster narrowness of outlook. But this much has to be conceded that, in some sense, we need authority to be anti-authoritarian and I think Islam does provide for that authority. No wonder, we are not even Mohammadans; we are Muslims – which means that our commitment is not to a *person* but to a particular *principle* – a principle to which the Prophet of Islam was himself committed being the first Muslim who acknowledged the validity of supreme doctrine that had called upon man to submit to God's Will.

Scholarly integrity is not only perfectly possible for a Muslim Scholar – it is a matter of paramount necessity. There is nothing he is called upon to renounce and till the very end of his search the tribunal to which he appeals is no other than the tribunal of reason. Did not the Holy Quran admonish the Prophet himself to ask the disbelievers to bring an argument if they were true:

hātu burhānakum in kuntum sādiqīn

Islam introduced liberalism in politics and sure enough it also stands for liberalism in education. Islam itself provided a charter of human liberty for the individual. Verily it came to make the individual free. Man was declared free to accept or reject Islam. There was to be no compulsion in religion. But the freedom it gave to mankind was possibly only if it submitted to the higher law – that is, the law which is in reality the law of man's own being. Education is liberal if it enables its votaries, nay qualifies them to *choose correctly things as well as means which*

74

are consistent with a great purpose for which man himself has been created. Unless the mind of man is liberated from negative emotions like suspicion, distrust, hatred, anger, ill-will and jealousy he is not liberated in the real sense of that term. The more an individual rescues himself from the grip of these negative forces the *more he comes into his own*. 'What are the attributes of man which qualify him for our esteem', is a question which is answered by Professor R. B. Perry, thus: 'What are the attributes of man which quality him for esteem, raise him above the level of the beasts, and give him that "dignity" which he claims and acknowledges? While there is a "humanism" which praises man for his *practical* achievements – for the history he has made – and worships the hero, whether he be conqueror or statesman, humanism in the educational sense praises man for his "spiritual" achievements. The mark of man in this high and estimable sense is not his *power*, but *his capacity to pursue ideals* – of truth, beauty and moral goodness. Construed as a cult of freedom, humanism signifies man's emancipation from the *limits of finitude* by the very act of discovering them.' It is in this sense that all liberal education is not merely a *branch* of education but education itself. In the last resort it resolves itself into a quest to the end that certain values (and these values may for the purpose of Islamic ideology be called *Quranic Values*) should pervade man's life and to an increasing extent manifest themselves in the activity, of not only the individual but also the larger synthesis of which he is a member – be it family, community or nation.

Chapter Four

The Islamic as Opposed to Modern Philosophy of Education

Hadi Sharifi

Hadi Sharifi, Professor of Philosophy and Sociology of Education of the University of Tehran, was born in Iran in 1937. He got his Ph.D. in Education from Heidelberg University. His publications include some valuable papers such as: *An Islamic View of Education*; *The Significance of Society in Islamic Education*; *Philosophy of Secondary Education*; *Education Problems of Modern Iranian Families*; *The Role of Education in the Quality of Life*.

From one point of view it is not fair to compare the traditional Islamic Philosophy of education, which is based on revelation, with modern philosophy of education by which is meant here purely humanistic and profane philosophies of education such as Idealism, Realism, Pragmatism, Marxism, Existentialism and Scientism. In the Islamic philosophy of education wisdom occupies a significant position, for wisdom (*hikmah*) – in the Quranic sense, namely: 'He gives the Wisdom to whomsoever He will, and who so is given the wisdom, has been given much good'[1] – leads in the light of revelation to the knowledge of *al-hakim* (the All-Wise), whereas in all the modern, rationalistic philosophies of education there is usually no room for wisdom[2] or intellect in its traditional sense.[3] But because modern and profane philosophies of education have become widespread, and have the better understanding of a traditional view of education, doubtless this comparison has a general character and does not itself deal with details. Nevertheless, it may shed some light upon contrasts and differences and a modern view of education. For aside from the use of human language for the explanation of their respective views, there is truly no common point between the two philosophies. One has a divine basis, and the other is the product of the limited human mind which either denies the revelation or is indifferent to the Truth.

As the history of traditional civilizations shows, the close connection between philosophy, science and religion is to be seen among all cultures. The significance of this connection lies in the fact that science and philosophy never transgress beyond a proper limit of curiosity and development, or are not suspended between those extremes, which lead to irremediable errors and contradictions. To these extremes belongs the prevalent attitude among modern scientists and philosophers, who insist upon the limited, rationalistic faculty of the human mind as the exclusive and only valid means of knowledge; and because of this presupposition they contradict themselves. For instance, when the *Realists* in the modern Western sense claim: 'Only the empirical world is real', or when any kind of knowledge which cannot be evaluated through the so-called scientific method is disapproved by modern scientists, one encounters an illogical and self-contradictory statement, by which the doors are closed to the possible and self-contradictory, because their presuppositions are nothing more than a dogmatic expression made by people who are not interested in dogmatics!

In connection with the already mentioned point, the following problem, which is common to all modern philosophies of education, should be discussed. Usually in all of them a certain aspect of human nature – it might be the social, material, individual, biological or psychological aspect – is taken as man's whole unique nature and being, and accordingly an educational theory is developed in which the unity and the comprehensive character of human nature is consequently neglected. Thus, modern philosophies of education are first of all short-lived; secondly, every philosophical view of education, because of its very limited and contingent standpoint, can be easily criticized, negated and finally replaced by another; and thirdly, conflicts and never-ending struggles among different philosophical ideas and speculations seem to be a natural phenomenon. But from a traditional point of view this situation is critical, for the simple reason that the sharp difference among the philosophical schools have brought confusion to the domain of educational theories, which usually try to define educational goals and orient the educational praxis.

The second problem, which will be dealt with here, is the problem of confusion among the educational aims and objectives in the modern world. This problem is apparently the result of a crisis in the value system, for if there is a relation between values and educational goals, then every goal, be it social, political, economical, etc., implicitly or explicitly originates from a value perception.[4] But the impact of this confusion on the domain of education praxis is the lack of agreement and harmony among the educators and parents on the one hand, and among psychologists, sociologists, economists and scientists on the other who are all interested in the education of children and youth – but each from his own specialized and limited point of view. The critic of this chaotic situation in modern industrialized society has stimulated two different attitudes. A group of scholars have expressed doubt if education necessarily must have aims.[5] And the second group support this postulate, that the science of education, like every other science, must be neutral to values. For the development of educational theory is one thing and the possibility of carrying it out is another.[6] Aside from the fact that the rejection of 'values' is in itself an expression of a certain value concept, neither of these two attitudes can throw light upon the dark and confused field of educational praxis. Consequently we are faced with two possibilities: either we have to restrict ourselves to extremely short-lived aims, which are practical and can be precisely described and formulated[7] (so that, for example, if honesty cannot be formulated in precise educational goals, it should be neglected!); or if we still insist on the pursuit of aims, which go beyond tomorrow or next week or next month, such as character building, we must agree to suffer from the lack of agreement among those interested and involved in educational discussions, and their failure to define right and wrong, ugly and beautiful. In the modern world the final purpose of man is not at all clear. Hence in matters of education no single approach is available either.[8]

Another characteristic of the modern philosophies of education lies in their insistence upon the rationalistic aspect of the human being and thus their forgetfulness of the position and significance of the heart in education, an amnesia which does not affect the educational ideas and actions of a traditional culture. The problem of a pure rationalistic attitude in education lies in the fact that, first of all, the human being in relation to his unity and comprehensive nature, is not purely a rationalistic creature, and much of his life – love, art and death – are not definable in a rationalistic way.[9] Above all, there is the very wonderful fact of human life itself, which can only be 'explained' as a miracle. Second, in educating our children, we have no right to concentrate our power and energy on one aspect of their existence and neglect the others. And finally the negligence of the position of the heart – the very centre of the human being, that which can realize the truth in education, amounts to the forgetfulness of the transcendental dimension of human life, to imprisonment in our limited sense perceptions and our wordly being forever, to confinement to areas which are by no means appropriate to our Intellect and real Nature (*Fitrah*).

To speak of the heart and its crucial importance in education as the only means of going beyond the ordinary level of consciouness and of realizing our real nature, is not understandable to the modern scientist and does not agree with the usual standards and norms of modern psychology only because modern science is limited to the empirical and the sensual. For a modern psychologist, the heart is not more than a bodily organ, which has a certain biological function; thus it seems to us necessary to explain through the words of Ghazālī, what traditional Muslims mean by the heart: 'When we speak of the heart, know that we mean the reality of man, which sometimes is called *ruh* (spirit) and sometimes *nafs* (soul); we do not mean that piece of flesh which lies in the left side of the chest; that organ is not worthy, for the cattle possess it, as do also the dead. It can be seen by the ordinary eyes, and whatever could be seen by eyes, belongs to this world, which is called the visible (*Shahadah*) world. The reality of the heart is not of this world; it has come to this world as a stranger or a passer-by, and that visible piece of meat is its vehicle and means, and all of the bodily features are its army, and it is the king of the whole body; the realization of God and the perception of His beauty is its function'.[10]

Paying attention to the position and the significance of the heart in education has been a common element in all traditional societies, and still is – so far as individuals have remained faithful to their tradition. But it is interesting that a man like Gandhi in his criticism of modern education, pointed out that 'It ignores the culture of the heart and the hand, and confines itself simply to the head'.[11]

Aside from the problem of existence of a gap between educational sciences and praxis, modern philosophical ideas and views could hardly be put into action or transformed into a way of life; in this respect all modern philosophies of education – be it Idealism, Pragmatism, Existentialism or whatever – are alike. How could Idealism, which claims 'reality is mind' be applied in life, when the empirical world stands there, and the Reality of Truth is Truth, absolutely independent of our mental perceptions? Or, how can one follow the Pragmatists, who define Truth in terms of practice or practical utility, when now at all times people before practising and before thinking of practical usefulness, search desperately to find a meaning for their action? Or, how can we speak of Existentialism, which postulates the freedom of the human being, as a way of life, when we see that our existence in this world is imposed upon us and we – as human beings – have no choice between coming and not coming into this world? It is not accidental that 'being born' is used as an intransitive verb in many languages. As Frithjof Schuon says: 'this man who "chooses himself", why does he not choose to be something other than what he has been chosen to be?'[12]

Of course, pointing to the fact that coming to this world – as well as going from this world – is not a human choice, does not imply believing in determinism. Nevertheless it seems clear that every philosophy of education in which there is no room for facts of life and death, and the justification of a meaning for the whole universe (these points belong to the domain of the metaphysical in its traditional sense), could hardly lead to harmony in educational endeavour, or to the filling of the gap between educational views and their satisfactory application.

On the contrary, the culture of a traditional society is dominated by harmony and unity; all branches of social life are deeply integrated. Education is an integral part of life[13] and so are philosophy and knowledge, and these are deeply interrelated. This close relation between philosophy, knowledge and education is of great significance in any traditional culture because the realization of the Ultimate Reality or the Absolute Truth occurs through the channel of spiritual training. The revelation of the existing spiritual doctrine usually provides a theoretical foundation, which describes the structure of Reality and the structure of human consciousness, the ontological status of the world and of all creatures, including human beings, and describes the way in which this reality is experienced by means of spiritual training. Because of this, there exists a sharp distinction between a traditional and a modern philosophy, and consequently between a traditional philosophy of education and a modern one. That the Reality can be realized through spiritual training, is accepted with complete certainty among all the great philosophies and religions of the world such as Taoism, Buddhism, Christianity and Islam.[14] The very existence of Sufi orders through the long life of Islamic civilization, and the spiritual ways in other traditions, through which countless ordinary people and intellectuals have realized the station of perfection and Truth, is witness to this fact. Because the realization of Truth by means of spiritual training is potentially open to every individual, the word of God pervades the whole culture, and so there remains no room for any kind of scepticism or agnosticism, and because of that Reality, unity and harmony appear in life. Values have a defined hierarchy, behaviour is structured, and stability appears on the scene of social life. This stability and also unity in a traditional culture are doubtless of a celestial nature; without the interference of God in our wordly life, unity (by which we do not mean uniformity) could never appear in social life, nor could this stability last for centuries, as is the case in Islamic civilization. If any further example is deemed necessary, one can compare the modern humanistic civilization of our age with the traditional civilization which existed before the Renaissance in Europe.

The lack of unity, harmony and stability in a culture works against the success of any worthy educational aim. But today many people really dislike stability and criticize the stable traditional societies as boring, tedious, out of date and unprogressive. We hear this voice now more often than a few decades ago even among young people, in the Islamic nations. Because this modern attitude among young people, which is influenced by Western thought, is one of the major educational problems in traditional societies, such as the Islamic, it needs further clarification here. In encountering the attack and critique made by modern thinkers concerning the so-called static situation of ancient traditional societies, one should keep in mind the following arguments: first, stability and change are two relative concepts and are not normative as such. In the modern world, change has been taken illogically as being automatically equivalent with the good and as a sign of progress. Yet, a storm is also dynamic and changes many things in its path. Why then does no one call a tornado 'positive and progressive'? In the case of a hurricane, 'change' means 'destruction' – but is this not also the case when modern thought changes or destroys a reasonable and worthy traditional way of life? Second, stability up to a certain degree is indispensable for the education of children. Severe and rapid change causes anxiety and insecurity in human beings, especially in children and young people. No real education can be successful in a society where values, behaviour, attitudes and aims change overnight. The chaotic situation in modern industrial nations is the result of this fact, that the stable centre of the culture has become eclipsed.[15] Everyone can offer whatever he wants to children and young people, and also to adults provided that he is clever enough to get a job as a teacher.

Third it is of crucial importance to notice that those social and philosophical schools like Marxism and Socialism, which support radical change and the restructuring of society, and attack severely the traditional stable societies, are striving paradoxically to establish a stable utopia, a classless society, which will attain everlasting peace.

81

What Marxists, materialists and socialists forget is the clear fact that their soulless utopia is an inverted image of the paradise of the religions in which, as the Holy Quran described it, 'are rivers of water unstalling, rivers of milk unchanging in flavour'.[16] But the soulless utopia of Marxism – if it could be by a sudden 'miracle' actualized! – is condemned to change, to break-down and to destruction, for it belongs to this world, and whatever belongs to this world cannot maintain itself eternally, for the simple reason that only the Truth, the Absolute can be eternal, according to the Quranic verse:

'All things perish, except His Face.'[17]

Finally, it is really absurd to deny that change takes place within a traditional society, although surely the purpose, kind and place of this change have not the same nature as in a modern society. Modern man, who is interested in outer change of a social, political and economic nature, experiences the shape and structure of his settlement, town, country and world as always changing – this process is called today development and progress. Changes in a traditional society however are directed towards the inner world of human beings, and nobody is exempted from this inner change except those who according to the Quran:

'have hearts, but understand not with them; they have eyes, but perceive not with them; they have ears, but they hear not with them. They are like cattle; nay, rather they are further astray. Those – they are the headless ones.'[18]

This inner change aims at the state of *al-insān al-kāmil* 'the perfect man' in Islamic education. Therefore that education is identified with a Way which has a beginning but not an end, for the beginning of this Way is the state of the human being as a terrestrial creature, hence limited and finite, but its end is the perfect man, who is *Khalīfat Allāh* (God's earthly vicegerent); this is the state of the primordial man, and because this state is identified with the realization of the Unity of Being, and hence the Truth as Absolute, the end of this Way is immersed in the Infinite.

Certainly not everyone in a traditional society can reach the state of the perfect man, but because in every traditional civilization there exists at least one perfect man who serves as a living example for those who are gifted and who decide to pursue the way of perfection, and because the Way of perfection is long and has different stages, corresponding to different human abilities and capacities, actually nearly everyone is engaged directly or indirectly in this striving.

Now, in this description, we have come to a point of vital significance in our social and cultural life today, concerning the encounter between tradition and modern, Western thought. We have taken as educational fact that everyone in a traditional civilization is engaged on some level in the way of inner perfection. This engagement absorbs the whole energy of a human being, who thus pays no attention to outer changes. To put it in another way, one might say that because traditional man (and woman) is concentrated on inner perfection, and because he thus attains satisfaction and happiness and clear meaning for his earthly life, he does not concentrate his energies upon the world outside and is not interested in outer changes or so-called development. Surely not everyone in a traditional society is aware of this – and it does not need to be the case – but the sages and holy men are absolutely aware of it. For they have realized in themselves a knowledge of metaphysical nature, which has enabled them to know who is man, what is the world, and what is the vocation of man in this world.

But those who have no idea of this change and the golden fruits of inner experience in a traditional society, imagine that traditional civilizations are static, and hence boring and unprogressive. Here, it seems necessary to point out that the striving towards perfection and self-realization does not by definition lead to the complete negligence of wordly affairs. Islamic civilization, as a living example, reveals to us the fact that even wordly activities – science, art, handicraft and technology – could be developed in a traditional atmosphere, which is full of the sense of Unity and Truth. According to S. H. Nasr: 'The unifying perspective of Islam has never allowed various forms of knowledge to be cultivated independently of each other. There has, on the contrary, always been a hierarchy of knowledge in which every form of knowledge from that of material substances to the highest metaphysics is organically interrelated, reflecting the structure of Reality itself.'[19]

Concerning development and progress, which the modern man so values, let us now put the question whether modern man has a better understanding of his nature than traditional man. We know that there are numerous theories and ideas, which try to define what man is. As Frithjof Schuon describes it:

'Modern thought is not in any definitive sense one doctrine among others; it is now the result of a particular phase of its own unfolding and will become what materialistic and experimental science or machines make it; no longer is it human intellect but machines – or physics, or chemistry, or biology – which decide what man is, what intelligence is, what truth is. Under these conditions man's mind more and more depends on the 'climate' produced by its own creations: man no longer knows how to judge as a man, in function, that is to say, of an absolute which is the very substance of the intelligence; losing himself in a relativism that leads nowhere, he lets himself be judged, determined and classified by the contingencies of science and technology; no longer able to escape from the dizzy fatality they impose on him and unwilling to admit his mistake, the only course left to him is to abdicate this human dignity and freedom. It is then science and machines which in their turn create man and, if such an expression may be ventured, they also 'create God' for the void thus left by dethroning God cannot remain empty, the reality of God and His imprint in human nature require a usurper of divinity, a false absolute which can fill the nothingness of an intelligence robbed of its substance.'[20]

Now, in this challenging situation, it seems helpful to describe the Islamic view of man, which clears the ground for a theoretical philosophy of education, though such an expression is not to be found in all the long history of Islamic thought on education.

Like the voice of the 'Adhān', which is all-embracing and transcendent, the Quranic image of man (*insān*) is clear, comprehensive and transcendent. The Quran, in a chapter which has the title *al-insān* 'Man', first refers to the metaphysical being of man, namely, man in a metatemporal time existing within Unity, or in the Absolute Being: 'Has there come on man a while of time when he was a thing unremembered?'.[21]

Before being created man existed in the knowledge of God. But because God's grace does not cease, according to the saying of Islamic mystics and philosophers, creation occurs. And so man becomes separated from his origin, and comes to this world as a stranger, and because of this separation he feels sad until he hears again the voice of God saying: 'return unto thy Lord'[22] According to Rumi: Everyone who is left far from his source wishes back the time when he was united with it.[23] Then the Quran points to the ontological aspect of man, as follows: 'We created man of a sperm-drop'.[24]

One of the essential points in the long centuries of the life of Islamic thought and education, a point which has actually moulded the entire Islamic attitude – is the very act of contemplation on the inexpressible wonder and miracle of creation in general and especially the creation of man. In relation to this point – as we mentioned at the beginning of this paper – wisdom (*hikmah*) occupies a high and significant position in the Islamic philosophy of education.

According to Muslim attitudes the human mind is impotent to perceive any relation and proportion between the microscopic sperm and wonder of the human form, if we overlook the hidden hand of the primordial Painter, who always and without interruption is acting according to the Quranic expression: 'every day he is upon some labour'.[25] We can detect His hand behind the miraculous scene of creation, provided that our intellect is not corrupted and clouded by pure human sentimentalities. Sadi the Persian poet and mystic, expresses this with the following words:

He gives the sperm a beautiful angelic face;
Who – if not God – has ever painted on water?[26]

The Muslims usually look at the phenomena of this world in a contemplative way. They say the very existence of knowledge, power and will in our world and the very existence of the faculties seeing and hearing in us, are not conceivable, unless they demonstrate the reality of the All-Knower. How can knowledge which is Quality, originate from blind matter, which is pure Quantity? The Quran says:

'We made him hearing, seeing.'[27]
'But you will not unless God wills; surely God is ever All-Knowing, All-Wise.'[28]

Muslims also know the laws of nature and the wonderful order of the universe, but all in all as Signs of God. The Quran refers to the law and order of the universe in the following way:

And a sign for them is the night; We strip it of the day and lo, they are in darkness. And the sun – it runs to a fixed resting-place; that is the ordaining of the All-mighty, the All-knowing. And the moon – We have determined it be stations, till it returns like an aged palm-bough. It behoves not the sun to overtake the moon, neither does the night outstrip the day, each swimming in a sky.'[29]

Or again:

'And we loose the winds fertilizing.'[30]

85

The Quran – not a Muslim scientist – speaks of the fertilizing winds at a time when nobody knew that winds are fertilizing! The Muslims argue accordingly, that if the sun and moon run in a ordained orbit, if the flowers grow from the dead land, and if the winds are fertilizing, to sum up, if there is law and order in nature and the universe, that is but because there is an Intelligent Being Who determines order and law. Were that not the case, or were there any other cause in nature and the universe than God, there must be disorder and confusion, as the Quran reminds us:

'. . . nor is there any God with Him; for them each God would have taken off that He created and some of them could have risen up over others.'[31]

Concerning modern thought, because man is interested only in the product of his own mind, the doors are open to all kinds of assumptions, as with the theory of evolution, which holds it possible that the result of a biological quantitative development – perhaps by way of chance! – ends in a qualitative consciousness. Schuon asks us to consider:

'the impossibility of demonstrating – or the absurdity of admitting – the possibility of a sudden burst of intellectual and moral objectivity in a process that is merely biological and quantitative.

For if a natural development were to lead up to a reflexive intelligence, to a sudden act of awareness that perceived the development for what it was, that outcome would be a reality falling entirely outside the realm of the revolutionary process; there would thus be no common measure between the act of awareness and the quite contingent movement that preceded it, and this movement therefore, under no circumstances, could be the cause of the awareness in question. This argument is the very negation of the theory of transformist evolution.'[32]

After the ontological aspect of man, attention is paid in Islam to the relation of man and God. This relation has two aspects, both of great significance from an educational point of view. In one aspect, the negative, man is a creature of restriction; in the other, positive, he partakes of the transcendent. According to the first, man is a forgetful being, because of his *nafs al-ammārah* (carnal soul), and as a result he may rebel against God. The Quran points to this human faith by saying:

'he has . . . forgotten his creation'[33]

and then asks:

'Does not man regard how that we created him of a sperm-drop? Then lo, he is a manifest adversary.'[34]

But the second aspect of this relation refers to man as 'the image of God' or as *Khalifat Allah* (viceroy of God). In this respect man is being created to comprehend all the Names and Qualities of God; therefore man can realise the Absolute, for

'. . . between two things, where is no substantial relation, there is no gnosis conceivable, therefore between the knower and the known must be a relation, and since the known, which is the Truth (God), is singular of essence and plural of attribute, so the man, which is a real knower is singular as an individual and plural so far as attributes, actions and faculties, according to the requirement of the Divine Wisdom, namely "God created man in his image".'[35]

The realization of the true nature of man, which is identified with man as 'image of God', is possible only by contemplation and prayer, according to the following verse, and also many other verses of the Quran:

'and serve thy Lord, until certainty comes to thee.'[36]

And this certainty, which comes direct from God, can be experienced in the heart and not in the mind, for the human brain can never escape its own limitations, its own agitations; but the human heart, when it is polished by the remembrance of God, can receive the grace of Heaven, and so realize the Truth. Hence the significance of the cultivation of the heart in Islamic education.

So wordly existence has in the Islamic philosophy of education a clear cause, a beginning, a meaning, a duration and finally an end, according to the verse:

'O, man, thou art labouring unto thy Lord laboriously, and thou shalt encounter Him.'[37]

Therefore the way of Islam is *sirat al-mustaqīm* (the straight way). But because of the modern system of education, and because of our contact with modern thoughts and philosophies, we have become alienated from our own traditional way of living and thinking. We have lost sight of the real meaning and significance of Islamic revelation, and the precious experiences of our ancestors in the light of revelation through fourteen centuries of the life of Islamic culture. And because of this unawareness, we are apt to forget the essential question, with which real intellectuals are concerned, within every sound traditional atmosphere, namely 'Who is Man?' Must we not first come to grips with this question before we take any action in the name of progress and change? For remember that even if we were able to harmonize and bring together the results of all those sciences, which in the modern world are engaged in research about human beings and human nature, such as biology, psychology, sociology, anthropology, etc., we would still fall short of attaining a clear picture of man; we could not say that we know who man is.

> 'In the face of the perils of the modern world, we ask ourselves; what must we do? This is an empty question if it be not founded upon antecendent certainties, for action counts for nothing unless it be the expression of a knowing and also a manner of being. Before it is possible to envisage any kind of remedial activity, it is necessary to see things as they are, even if, as things turn out, it costs us much to do so; one must be conscious of those fundamental truths that reveal to us the values and proportions of things. If one's aim is to save mankind, one must first know what it means to be a man; if one wishes to defend the Spirit, one must know what is Spirit; "Before doing, one must be" says the proverb; but without knowing, it is impossible to do.'[38]

Traditional vis-a-vis Modern Education: Need for a New Perspective

Chapter Five

A Plea for a Modern Islamic University: Resolution of the Dichotomy

S. M. Hossain

Syed Moazzam Hossain was born in Bengal in 1901 and educated at Dacca and then at Oxford University from where he got his D.Phil. in Arabic in 1929. He joined Dacca University as Reader in Arabic and Islamic Studies in 1930, became the Professor and Head of this Department and later the Vice-Chancellor of Dacca University and retired in 1953. As Chairman of 'Arabic Islamic University Commission' he submitted a plan for the establishment of an Islamic University which is now being set up. At present he is Professor Emeritus of Dacca University. His publications include a critical study with translation of early Arabic poetry – *Early Arabic Odes*; *Editio Princeps* of al-Hakim al-Naisabiai; *Kitab Marifat ulum al-Hadith*.

The education of Muslims should include training not merely for acquiring knowledge and skills in order to be fit for entering one or other careers open to educated young men for earning money and position to live comfortably and honourably in their transient wordly life; it should emphasize training for fostering the innate Islamic instinct with which every child is born, as stated in a well-known authentic Tradition of the Holy Prophet (S). The first and foremost function is to sow the seeds of this instinct in the seed-bed of this world so that its saplings are transplanted in the garden abode to blossom with bliss and beatitude for their eternal life in the next world.

The Quran is the first Book in which mankind is exhorted to attain perfection by acquiring knowledge through reading and writing. The frequent mention of writing, reading and the pen in the Quran and particularly in the very first revelation of the Prophet (S), is rather amazing since it is a well-known fact that not only was the use of writing a rare novelty in Arabia then, but the Prophet (S) was himself unacquainted with writing and reading. The revelation was granted to the Prophet (S) to bring him, and through him the whole of humanity, to perfection. Imbued with this spirit, Muslim scholars applied themselves to develop an elaborate system of education which produced men capable of undertaking responsibilities of this world and the world hereafter. They developed this system as a result of the teaching of the Quran – the mission of the Prophet Muhammed (S). They could not have drawn any inspiration from the pre-Islamic Arabs, for the development of a tradition of systematic education as 'the cultural and economic level of the nomad population in the pre-Islamic time was, as it has always been, too low to support any literary effort', (F. Rosenthal, *History of Muslim Historiography*, Leiden, 1952, p. 16). In this connection the opinion of the German scholar Moritz Cantor is quoted: 'That a people who for centuries together were closed to all the cultural influences from their neighbours, who themselves did not influence others during all this time, who then all of a sudden imposed their faith, their laws, and their language on other nations to an extent which has no parallel in history – all this is such an extraordinary phenomenon that it is worthwhile to investigate its causes. At the same time we can be sure that this sudden outburst of intellectual maturity could not have originated of itself.' (H.M.P., Vol. ii, pp. 1277–78). If one had really investigated that cause of the 'sudden outburst of intellectual maturity' of the Arabs, one must have realized that it was due to the revolution caused by Islam in the whole outlook of the people. By making it incumbent upon the believer to acquire knowledge and by enjoining upon him to observe and to think for himself, Islam created an unbounded enthusiasim for acquiring knowledge amongst its followers. Florian Cajori, in his *History of Mathematical Notation*, describes the result of this revolution in the following words: 'The Arabs present an extraordinary spectacle in the history of civilization, unknown, ignorant, and disunited tribes of the Arabian Penisula, untrained in government and war, are, in the course of ten years, fused by the furnace-blast of religious enthusiasm into a powerful nation. A hundred years after this grand march of conquest, we see them assume the leadership of intellectual pursuit; the Muslims become the great scholars of their time.'

Under this stimulus of the Islamic injunctions for acquiring knowledge, the Arabs and other Muslim peoples turned to the learning of the various branches of knowledge, preserving and improving upon the heritage left by preceding civilizations and enriching every subject to which they turned their attention.

The Attitude of Islam towards Knowledge

The Quran:

None can grasp the message of revelation except men of understanding and those firmly grounded in knowledge. (iii, 7, 8, vi. 105; xxii, 54; xxiv, 6). Allah bears witness that there is no God but He, and the angels and the men endowed with knowledge, established in righteousness (iii, 16). Lack of true knowledge leads people to revile the true God, (vi, 108); invent lies against Him, and worship other gods besides Him (xxii, 71). The only safety lies in following the revelation which is replete with the knowledge of God (xi, 14). Whosoever has been given knowledge has indeed been given abundant good (ii, 269). Only those people will be promoted to suitable ranks and degrees who have faith and are possessed of knowledge (iviii, ii) and only those who have knowledge really fear God and tread the path of righteousness (xxxv, 28). Say, 'are those who possess knowledge and those who do not possess knowledge, on equal footing?' (xxxix, 9). And say, O my Lord, increase me in knowledge, (xx,114). Noah, David and Solomon possessed knowledge (xxviii, 14). Jacob had a lot of knowledge and experience (xii, 68); Joseph possessed abundant power and knowledge (xii, 22); and so also was Moses given wisdom and knowledge (xxviii, 14). An idea of the immense incentive provided in the Quran for the cultivation of learning and reasoning can be formed from the constant exhortations in it to believers to know, to see, to observe, to think, to ponder and to deduce.

The Hadith

The Prophet's devotion to knowledge and his teachings on its supreme value and importance place him above all other teachers and bring him into the closest affinity with the modern world of thought. He said: 'Should the day come wherein I increase not in knowledge wherewith to draw nearer to God, let the dawn of that day be accursed.'

'He dies not who seeks knowledge.'

'Seeking after knowledge is obligatory for every Muslim.'

'Seek knowledge even though in China.'

'He, who leaves his home in search of knowledge, walks in the path of Allah, Lo! The angels offer their wings to the seekers of knowledge.'

'To be present in a circle of learned men is better than prostrating oneself in prayer a thousand time or visiting a thousand sick persons and attend a thousand funerals'. It was then said, 'O, Apostle of Allah, is it better than the reading of the Quran?' to which he replied, 'what good, though, is the Quran except through knowledge?'

'A word of wisdom is like the lost treasure of a believer who has got the best right to secure it wherever he might have found it.'

'An hour's contemplation and study of God's creation is better than a year of adoration.'

'Acquire knowledge, he who acquires it in the way of Allah performs an act of piety; he who speaks of it praises the Lord; he who seeks it adores God, he who dispenses instruction in it bestows alms; he who imparts it to the deserving persons performs an act of devotion.'

'A father can confer on his children nothing more valuable than the gift of education, it is better that a man should secure a good education for his children than he should leave a treasure of gold and silver for them.'

There are hundreds of sayings of the Prophet (S) in which the supreme value of knowledge is taught. The Prophet (S) not only inculcated the necessity and value of knowledge but also urged the cultivation of the scientific spirit of reasoning, enquiry and investigation.

The study of the Quran and Hadith, the twin fountainhead of knowledge, created all the impulse and impetus for the cultivation and advancement of Islamic learning.

The Concept and Classification of Knowledge

'He grants wisdom to whom He pleases, And who is granted wisdom, he indeed is given a great boon. And none mind but men of understanding.' (The Quran, ii, 269). According to Ibn Khaldun, wisdom and philosophy are identical. The ideal wisdom or philosophy is the knowledge of facts, ideals and values. Knowledge is of three kinds: (i) knowledge by inference (*ilm al-yaqin*), (ii) knowledge by perception (*'ain* al-yaqin), and (iii) knowledge by personal experience of intuition (haqq al-yaqīn).

The first type of knowledge depends either on the truth of its presupposition as in deduction, or on its probability as in induction; the second is either scientific knowledge based on observation and experiment or historical knowledge based on reports and descriptions of actual experiences; and the third is the outcome of inner or personal experiences.

According to al-Maturidi, sources of knowledge are three: (1) Sense-organs (al-a'yan), (ii) Reports (al-akhbar) and (iii) Reasons (al-nazr). (Kitab al-Tawhid, Mss. Cambridge).

The Ikhwan al-Safa, instead of Reports (al-akhbar) accepted the esoteric doctrine of the way of initiation and authority as a source of knowledge. (Rasail, iii, pp. 42, 228, 322, 384).

According to Ibn Bajjah, human knowledge is of two kinds: (i) Knowledge based on proof and (ii) Knowledge based on direct experience through religious devotion and given by God, i.e. intuitive knowledge. This second method is that of the Sufis, notably of al-Ghazali, and it enables one to gain knowledge of God.

Ibn Rushd, in his Tailkhis Kitab al-Nafs, elaborately discussed this issue and classified knowledge into individual and universal knowledge (pp. 8–67).

Al-Farabi has closely identified knowledge with philosophy. He has devoted a whole treatise to its elaboration, 'On the Different Meanings of the Intellect', which had a wide circulation in the Middle Ages and was translated into Latin. He classifies it into practical knowledge which deduces what should be done, and theoretical which helps the soul to attain perfection. The latter is again classified into material, habitual and acquired (Al-Thamarat al-Mardiyyah, p. 54).

In his Tahdhib al-Akhlaq, Miskawaih classifies human faculties into three: the highest reason, the lowest is appetite, and between the two lies courage. Man is man by the first. Therefore, perfection belongs especially to the rational soul. Here (pp. 67–78) he has dwelt at length on the education of children and youth.

Contrary to al-Farabi, Alexander and Aristotle, Ibn Sina holds that the potential knowledge in man is an indivisible, immaterial and indestructible substance, although it is generated at a definite time and as something personal to each individual. He rejects the general and especially later Greek doctrine of the absolute identity of subject and object in intellectual operation.

The Ikhwan al-Safa, who were very much interested in epistemology, divided all branches of knowledge into three major classes: mathematics, physics and metaphysics.

Mathematics included the Theory of numbers, geometry, astronomy, geography, music, theoretical and practical acts, ethics and logic (*Rasail*. i, pp. 23–362). Physics included matter, form, motion, time, space, the sky, generation, minerals, the essence of nature, plants, animals, the human body, the senses, life and death, microcosm, pleasure, pain and language (*Rasail*, ii, pp. 3–388, iii, pp. 3–181). Metaphysics was subdivided into psychorationalism and theology. The first one included psychics, rationalitics, being, macrocosm, mind, great years, love, resurrection and causality (*Rasail*, iii, pp. 182–371). Theology included faith, divine law, prophethood, call unto God, the incorporeals, politics, the structure of the world, magic and friendship (*ibid*, iii, pp. 373–432, vi, 3–478).

According to al-Ghazali, perfection of the soul consists in knowledge, albeit intuitive knowledge. Knowledge of the sciences dealing with things that God has made is regarded by al-Ghazali as a necessary prelude to the knowledge of God himself. The study of all branches of knowledge and taking the greatest share of most of them is a necessary part of the mystic discipline. 'If the soul has not been exercised in the sciences dealing with fact and demonstration, it will acquire mental phantasms which will be mistaken by it to be truths descending upon it.' (cf. *Mīzān al-A'māl*, pp. 35, 36; *Ihya*, part 1, Book I, Section 7 on *'Aql*).

In bringing closer together the theological and cosmological traditions and in studying nature with a view to discovering God's wisdom in creation, al-Ghazali was the precursor while Fakhr al-Din Razi advanced upon a path already trodden by his friend. His encyclopedic work, *The Jami 'al 'Ulum*, written for Khwarizm Shah Abu al-Muzaffar ibn Malik al-Mu'azzam, on the Muslim sciences, offers a good account for the classifications, definitions, and scope of the various Muslim sciences. The book begins with a discussion on *traditional religious sciences* such as theology, jurisprudence, dialectics, comparative religion, inheritance, will and testament, Quranic commentary, and reading of the Quran and Hadith; and then it discusses *The linquistic sciences* dealing with grammar, syntax, etymology of words, prosody and poetic metre and, after that, history. After the transmitted (*naqli*) *sciences* Imam Razi devotes the rest of the book to the *intellectual* (*aqli*) *sciences* which include natural philosophy, interpretation of dreams, physiognomy, medicine, anatomy, pharmacology, the science of the occult properties of things, alchemy, theurgy, agriculture, geometry, the science of weights, arithmetic, algebra, optics, music, astronomy, astrology, metaphysics, ethics and its various branches and even chess and other games, (cf. H.M.P., Vol. I, p. 651).

Ibn Khaldun classified sciences into natural (*tabi'iyyah*), rational (*'aqliyyah*), legal, transmitted or positive sciences based on the divine law, and the philosophic sciences. According to him, positive sciences are the special property of a particular religious community while the philosophic sciences are those which a human being can understand by virtue of the nature of his thought and the subjects, the problems, the ways of demonstration, and the modes of teaching to which he is guided by perception. Again, he classified the philosophic sciences into four fundamental groups of sciences: Logic, mathematics, physics and metaphysics or the Divine Science. In this respect Ibn Khaldun has followed in the footsteps of Ibn Rushd.

It is noteworthy that the Muslims made invaluable contributions in almost all branches of human knowledge. Universities, observatories and all other centres of learning in Muslim countries included these branches of learning in their syllabi and courses of studies. It may not be out of place to mention that the Shi'ite scholar Nasir al-Din Tusi made the celebrated Maraghah observatory a 'splendid assembly' of the men of knowledge and learning by making special arrangements for the teaching of philosophical sciences, besides mathematics and astronomy, and by providing a huge library containing more than four hundred thousand volumes. (Cf. *Hukama-i-Islam*, Vol. II. p. 256; *Yadnameh-i-Tusi*, p. 66; Browne, *Literary History of Persia*, Vol. II p. 456).

Traditionally, Islamic learning is distinguished between two classes: the sciences which are connected with body or matter and those which are connected with spirit and ideas; again it is classified in respect of acquisition into the sciences which are connected with the Quran and those which the Muslims learnt from foreign peoples. The former class includes the religious sciences and the linguistic sciences; in the latter are the sciences of the foreigners or the ancient sciences. The two terminologies, Traditional (*naqliyya*) Sciences and Intellectual (*'Aqliyya*) Sciences, which also revert to the Religious Sciences and the Ancient Sciences, are of very late origin.

The general scope of this division may be shown as follows:

I. *The Religious Sciences:*

1. Quranic Recitation,
2. Quranic Exegesis,
3. Apostolic Tradition,
4. Jurisprudence,
5. Scholastic Theology,
6. Arabic Grammar,
7. Lexicography,
8. Rhetoric & Prosody,
9. Literature.

II. *The Foreign Sciences:*

1. Philosophy,
2. Geometry,
3. Astronomy,
4. Music,
5. Medicine,
6. Chemistry,
7. Mathematics,
8. Physics,
9. Magic.

Courses of Study and Institutions.

The greatest teacher the world has ever seen is the Prophet of Islam, whose scintillating knowledge and inspiring instruction struck sparks into the hearts of his Companions and Followers – sparks that at once glowed in the minds of the Muslims into such a burning desire for knowledge and learning as made them masters of a vast empire and teachers of medieval Europe.

The entire teaching system of the Muslims fell into two groups, the elementary and the higher education. In both was conspicuously present from the outset, that elaborate system of instruction which we have in our schools, colleges, universities and other educational institutions, governed by a set course of studies, controlled by regulations of all kinds and subject to official supervision. In the Muslim educational system is revealed a magnificent experiment of public enterprise in education, free public instruction, freedom of teaching and freedom of studies – an amazing anticipation of the most modern conception and experimentation in education. Here the State had very little to do in the beginning, and at a later date it came forward only to supplement the public efforts for the diffusion and promotion of learning, and extended necessary financial support without imposing, however, any restriction and control in the matter of teaching.

There was no fixed rule as to the number and period of lectures and holidays. All these depended on the inclination or discretion of teachers. As for example, 'Abdullah bin Abbas lectured one day apiece on the interpretation of the Quran law, the Muslim conquests, poetry and the works of the Arabs; Hasan al-Basri was in the habit of teaching till past midday; Shafi'i began at dawn with the Quran and went on till noon with classes in tradition, discussion, Arabic grammar and poetry.

The early Muslim educationists fully realized the great importance of rapport between teachers and the taught. They were well aware of the moulding and enlivening effect of such rapport with the students and the enduring influence it leaves behind throughout student lives. Their method of instruction was a combined form of tutoring, advising and group discussion in the college as well as in the house or halls of residence of students as in modern European and American Universities.

In all the stages of development of Islamic education, the teacher held the same independent position. In this system of education, teachers were the fountain-head; degrees were valued because of them, contrary to the modern practice, where the teacher is a paid employee and the institution is the employer, and where the teacher has no role in conferring degrees except through examining scripts. Hence the value of degrees varies with the institution, but in the Islamic system of education not only the value of degrees but also that of the institution itself rest on the merit and scholarship of the teacher.

The house of Arqam was the first seat of Islamic learning for the education of the Companions, and after the migration to al-Madina, the Prophet (S), besides his mosque – which was built as a place of prayer as well as instruction for his followers – used to teach at al-Suffa. After his death, his Companions followed the same practice; and in the Masjid-i-Nabawi, Hadrat 'Ayesha, 'Abdullah bin 'Umar and Zayd bin Thabit used to teach; and in the mosque at Mecca 'Abdullah bin

'Abbas used to teach lessons. With the expansion of Islam, mosques were built in every important place and city and classes were opened in them.

The system of education in the mosque, inaugurated by the Prophet (S) and expanded by his Companions, created a wonderful drive for adult education amongst the Muslims. It was organized on a purely voluntary basis and given entirely free.

In many mosques there were different halls and annexes to provide accommodation for classes as well as residence for students and teachers. To the builders of even the earliest mosques goes the glory of establishing colleges along with the Houses of God. The big mosque in a large city which had invariably a big college attached to it is the *Jami'*, from which the term *Jami'a* has later been derived as the name for a University.

Separate institutions for higher studies called (sing.) Madrasah did not come into being until 350 A.H. Of the numerous Madrasahs which filled Bagdad, Nisapur, Cairo and other cities of the Muslims, Nizamiya, Mustansiriya, Azhar, Dar al-'llm, Dar al-Hikmat, Madrasah-i-Abu 'Ali al-Husain of Nisapur were prominent. Not only theological subjects were taught in these Madrasahs but also Faculties of Medicine, Philology, Applied Sciences and so on were established.

A Madrasah for women was established in Cairo in 634 A.H. by the daughter of Mamluk Sultan Tahir. The daughter of Malik Ashraf, known as Khatun, erected a women's Madrasah in Damascus. Another Madrasah was founded by Zamurrad, wife of Nasiruddin of Aleppo.

After the creation of Madrasahs as separate institutions, in many cases the mosque itself was used for the purpose of teaching. Moreover, every great mosque built by the Muslim emperors had a full-fledged Madrasah attached to it. A chapel and a library were necessary components and residential arrangements for students and teachers were a distinctive feature of the Madrasahs, which were thus precursors of the residential colleges of British Universities.

The system of education in the old Indian Madrasahs was more or less the same as was in vogue in the countries of the Turkish Empire, and it had the same objective as the countries of Central Asia which disseminated that system. Thus, under the Afghans, the Turks and the Moghuls, the courses of study were :– (1) Grammar, (2) Rhetoric, (3) Law, (4) Jurisprudence, (5) Logic, (6) Mysticism (7) Exegesis, (8) Tradition and (9) Medicine which included some branches of science, such as alchemy, botany, and biology. During the reign of Akbar, the syllabus also included some new subjects such as agriculture, economics, civics and history. This system of education continued till the British occupied the Sub-continent. After their military victory and in order to perpetuate their rule, they practised a policy of 'divide and rule', but the existing system of education proved to be a deterrent. They then introduced a new system which was opposed by the Muslims but it was imposed. The present system of education – secular or religious – is the direct outcome of that scheme which was designed to serve the colonial design of the British. By dividing education into secular and religious education and by establishing separate institutions for both divisions, the British scheme of dual education replaced the unitary Islamic system of education resulting in perennial discord among the products of the two systems.

The Modern Islamic University

The mosque was the university of Islam in the great days, and it deserved the name of *university* since it welcomed to its precincts all the knowledge of the age and attracted scholars from every quarter. All education was brought into the religious sphere. There was no such term in Islam as the 'profane sciences', for it includes the whole sphere of man's activities. The impulse to scientific study was created among the Muslims by the Quran bidding them to observe the phenomena of nature; the alternation of day and night, the properties of earth, air, fire and water, the mysteries of birth and death, growth and decay and the like. The study of the Quran led them to the use of the inductive method which paved the way to most modern discoveries.

The system of liberal education as imparted in the mosque was also followed in the separate institutions, which came to be established, beside and outside it, under the name of *Madrasah*. Islam, having first opened the path to learning, naturally retained the primacy of its own sciences in the Madrasahs, but other branches of learning that were taught in the mosques were also cultivated with equal zeal. The Madrasahs or the Muslim Universities were no doubt different from those of modern times, but they were enlightened institutions that led the world in learning and research. The great professors of those universities were teachers of modern Europe.

101

The *Studia* of mediaeval Europe were just imitations of Madrasahs both in their name and free growth. The great Muslim Madrasah was also the archetype of the *Studium General* which, with the later requisite of the royal or papal authorization, came to be known as University in Europe.

The devastating inroads made by the hoards of Ghenghiz Khan destroyed the most important universities and massacred the learned. This havoc dealt a severe blow to Islamic learning which, although it no doubt continued to survive, paralyzed the pristine Islamic spirit of liberal study and investigation.

The European nations which had been led to the pursuit of knowledge and science by the inspiring examples of the Muslims, achieved wonderful advancement in the intellectual as well as political fields just as the Muslims themselves did when they faithfully followed the teachings of the Quran for the cultivation of knowledge. But the Muslims later abandoned the study of natural sciences denouncing them as impious, being the knowledge of infidels, whereas the early Muslims acquired all ancient knowledge although it was the knowledge of a heathen race. The Quran urges the Muslims to assuage the miseries of mankind; but for want of scientific and technological knowledge to mitigate the evils of poverty, disease, squalor and low standard of living among the masses, the Muslims have, to that extent, failed to carry out the explicit injunction of the Quran.

Muslims all over the world are now realizing the paramount need for scientific studies. Technological advance, no less than theoretical science, is invaluable for acquiring power over nature and, therefore, the present emphasis on it in every Muslim state is most welcome. There is an ever-increasing desire in the Muslim world today to root out social and moral evils and to build a new society on sound Islamic moral foundations. But the desire is yet far from realization and the process of moral regeneration is much slower than that of an intellectual revival. It is much more difficult to mould the character of a nation than to mould its thought. What is now needed most is Islamic ideology and the moulding of life in accordance with this ideology. All that is required is to bring its moral values home to every Muslim through universal education. Islamic ideology and Islamic practice are not the same. One is an affair of the intellect, the other is that of the will. An enlightened intellect is not necessarily a dedicated will. A wide gulf between belief and practice is seen today throughout the Muslim world. True revival of Islamic culture depends mainly upon the bridg-

102

ing of this gulf: the yawning gulf between the secular and religious systems of education which led to an unfortunate clevage in Muslim society. A modern Islamic university, laying a foundation of an eventually unified system of education, will bridge the gulf between the two systems of education and turn out well-educated young men endowed with Islamic character and, as such, will prove themselves worthy and useful citizens of the Islamic World.

Chapter Six

Traditional Islamic Education – Its Aims and Purposes in the Present Day

M. A. Zaki Badawi

Muhammad Aboulkhir Zaki Badawi was born in Egypt in 1922. After maktab where he memorized the Quran, Zaki Badawi took the degrees of Al-Aliyah and Al-Alimiyah from Al-Azhar. He then took B.A. (Hons) in psychology and Ph:D. from the University of London. He then returned to Al-Azhar as a teacher.

From Al-Azhar, Zaki Badawi went to teach at the Muslim College of Malaya, then joined the University of Singapore, and later the University of Malaya in Kuala Lumpur. Twelve years ago he moved to Nigeria. There, until recently, he was Professor of Islamic Studies at Abdullahi Bayero College, Ahmadu Bello University, Kano. At present he is the Director of the Islamic Culture Centre, London.

Muslim educators unanimously agree that the purpose of education is not to cram the pupil's minds with facts but to prepare them for a life of purity and sincerity. This total commitment to character-building based on the ideals of Islamic ethics is the highest goal of Islamic education.[1]

Muslim society naturally must aim at instilling the principles of Islam in the hearts and minds of its young to achieve through them the ideal of the faith, the continuity of the *Ummah* which the Holy Quran describes as 'the best nation ever brought forth to men'.[2] The *Ummah* was so described not for its superiority in knowledge or skill but for the fact that it enjoined virtue and forbade vice and believed in Allah.[3]

Some educational systems emphasize education for individual excellence. The interests and goals of society as a whole are secondary to those of the individual in such a system. The Sophists of ancient Greece formulated and defended this outlook. But there are those who take the opposite stand and subordinate the interests and goals of the individual to those of society. The clearest example of this attitude is that of Sparta. There, the sole-purpose of education was to submerge individual identity into the totality of the group.

Islam effected a balance between the two tendencies. Individual excellence was not sacrificed for the good of the group nor was the goal of the group given second place to that of the individual.

This balance runs through all aspects of Muslim education and is manifested most strikingly in the area of its aims and purposes. To illustrate this more forcefully we may use Max Weber's analysis of the types of education. He enumerates three types. The first he calls 'charismatic education' which is dominant 'in periods in which religion reaches its highest point'. It aims at awakening 'religious intuition and the inner readiness for transcendental experience'. The predominant aim in this case 'is not the transfer of specific content or skill but to stir up certain innate powers'. This type is perhaps exemplified by what the Sufis call 'tarbiyah'. It is concerned primarily with the individual's inner excellence.

The second and very different type is 'education for culture'. It is based on 'the belief that certain contents perceived as classical have the inner qualifications of breeding a certain social type. It is not only the substance which is valued but the style of life which unconsciously will be transferred through the ideas presented. Not the content as such but its formative educational power is being stressed. Good examples are the creation of the gentleman or of the Chinese mandarin who acquire through the study of the classics a certain mental mood, style of thought, and inner disposition and sentiment.' The emphasis here is on social distinction.

The third type is 'specialist education'. It 'seeks to transfer a special knowledge or skill and is strictly correlated with the growth of division of labour which makes the specialist indispensable in modern industrial society.' This type is exemplified by the training given in some of the modern secular trade schools where the whole relationship is purely mechanical and lacking the inner depth of charismatic education and the concern for the human personality characteristic of the cultural education.[4]

Islam blends the three types in its own system giving prominence to inner purity to be manifested in social consciousness and idealistic endeavour towards the mastery of any skill to which the person has assigned himself.

Traditional Muslim education was not an activity separated from other aspects of society. It acted in harmony with all other activities and institutions to confirm them and to be reinforced by them. Not surprisingly, the mosque, the heart of all religious activities, was the apex of the whole system. Neither the educator nor the student was isolated from the rest of the community. They more often than not combined other functions with that of education, thus retaining their close contact with everyday life. There was always a close personal relationship between the teacher and the student which ensured that moral and spiritual guidance was given alongside the teaching of various skills.

Success was, of course, important, but failure did not turn the individual into a useless burden on society. Whatever he had learnt, and however little, would still be of value and his place within society would still be guaranteed.

The level of achievement of the student in the traditional system was measured by the totality of the student as a person. His piety and moral conduct was regarded as of equal, or indeed superior, importance to his attainment in other spheres.

The core subject in traditional education was the Holy Quran. The study of the Quran was the preoccupation of the traditional school from the very moment that it came into being.[5]

The education of the Muslim child began with the Holy Book which he learnt to read, recite and memorize. The Holy Quran is the final guide for the Muslim in matters of basic beliefs, forms of worship and rules of conduct. We are enjoined by Allah and His Prophet (peace be upon Him) to benefit from learning and teaching it.[6] From the study of the Quran, the student develops his knowledge of Islam and derives his moral ideal.

The first stage in Islamic formal education was the maktab or *kutab* which has adhered to this curriculum up to the present time.[7] Throughout the Muslim world, regardless of religious doctrine, school of law, racial composition or language, the curriculum is the same. An Indonesian, Nigerian, Pakistani or Saudi child learns the same things.

The maktab was the equivalent of the primary school, the madrassah was the intermediate stage and the mosque was the apex of the system. It was, and still is, the university of Muslim education. The most famous of these mosque universities is Al Azhar of Cairo.

Being very much a part of the community, the mosque university kept an open door for all comers to participate in the learning activities and in their general educational endeavour. Students attended and left on their own accord. They were not coerced but acted on their own inclination.

Young children had, however, to be made to attend the maktab and a certain degree of coercion and discipline was exercised to enhance their motivation.[8] Al-Qabisi, who died in 403 A.H. (1012 A.D.), argued that every Muslim child should be sent to the maktab by his parents; but he did not feel that it was the function of the state to enforce such attendance.[9] This stemmed from the general view of Muslim jurists as to the role of the political power in everyday life. A great many obligations were left to the conscience of the individual and the general concern of the community without the interference of the state. Moral authority has always been rated higher than legal power in the concept of Muslim social organization.[10]

The promotion of students did not take place through the mechanical examination system which is so familiar to us.

The teacher assessed the student's progress and determined the next step to be taken. The student himself, if able, assisted in this exercise. Each student, therefore, was free to attain his ultimate level in any of the areas of his interest without being held back because of difficulties in subsidiary or extraneous disciplines.[11]

Training in the mosque university was a combined activity in which both student and teacher took part. The student had to be persuaded rather than instructed and the teacher had to argue his case rather than dictate it. In this way, the personality and the intellectual ability of the student was allowed to develop and grow.

Unlike the modern system which operates like a factory with a production line measuring its success by statistical tables, traditional Islamic education measured its activity by the fact that it stimulated the community as a whole to take an interest in the higher issues so fundamental to its nature and survival.

Because of his role in the community and in the field of education, the teacher acted not simply as the guide to better knowledge but also as the example to better conduct. Teaching was not simply a profession to be sold but a role to be fully and completely performed.

In all this it can be seen that the school reflected most faithfully the society.

The able and studious were allowed to move forward at their own speed not restricted by a rigid curriculum nor herded in their age groups. In the same class pupils of different ages and different abilities sat side by side and took part in the exhilarating activities. The dull benefited from the brilliant and the able understood and appreciated both the difficulties and the merits of the slow learner. But above all, the school, like the mosque, was classless. Students from all classes of society sat together at the feet of the same scholar.[12] Only by their contribution to the activities of the group were they distinguished.

Early in Islam teaching was regarded as a religious duty and the teacher was therefore barred from accepting fees.[13] When institutions of learning made their appearance the jurists found a way to legalize the payment of fees and also to specify the duties and rights of teacher and pupil.[14] Direct payment by the student to teacher, however, was restricted to the early stages of education (the maktab) and only where endowments were not available. At the level of the madrassah and mosque, teachers were often provided for by large endowments and gifts given by rulers and men of wealth. A scholar was therefore assured of a living wherever he went. It was indeed customary for the scholar to traverse the Islamic world from one end to the other without difficulty receiving maintenance on the way from various educational institutions in recognition of some teaching given or received. It was not uncommon for the teacher to become a student in one and the same institution. For he following the instruction of the Prophet (peace be upon Him) sought knowledge throughout his life 'from the cradle to the grave'. In this way he learnt by direct and recent experience how the learning process operated.

Teaching was not a profession acquired by a mere certificate awarded by a government body, but something achieved by real ability and true vocation. To be sure, there were Ijazahs (licences) given to students on completion of their studies of a particular work authorizing them to teach it. The value of such a licence depended on the prestige of the teacher who issued it. The Ijazah, however, was not the final qualification; the teacher had to prove himself a worthy leader of his pupils.

The curriculum of the maktab as stated earlier centred around the Quran and the child was taught to read it and learn it by heart. He also learnt to read, write and calculate and in some areas of the Muslim world was taught Arabic language and literature so as to enhance his appreciation of the Holy Quran and the Tradition of the Prophet.[15] A great deal of the learning had to be by rota involving drills and repetition, sometimes at the expense of understanding. Once the Holy Book and a fair number of Hadiths had been mastered the student was involved in courses of exegesis and scholarly elaboration of the Tradition.

Such activity encompassed the whole field of Islamic knowledge. For around these two sources, the Holy Quran and Tradition, revolves everything else, whether law, theology, mysticism or rituals. In discussing any problem of life or faith the student and the teacher must rest their arguments finally on the divine source, the Holy Quran.

Other disciplines not bearing directly on Islamic studies were not neglected or excluded from the system. Medicine and science and other technical knowledge were learnt through apprenticeship. The student having been through the maktab and having already acquired basic religious knowledge was able to satisfy his interest in the healing profession or in any other skill by joining with a master to teach and guide him. The objective here was not divorced from the main objective of society, namely the Islamic ethical principles and values. In the circles of Muslim medical men and engineers and mathematicians and philosophers, the final aim remained decidedly religious. For every action and every endeavour had to be justified in religious terms.[16] Thus, the professional standards of excellence and the ethical standards of professional conduct were reinforced and safeguarded by religious ethics and values.

To summarize, I would like to make the following comparisons between the traditional system and the modern:

1. Traditional education was an integral part of its own society. The educational institutions were natural developments springing from the society, responding to its needs and responsive to its demands. There was no universal compulsory educational system, no imposition from above. In contrast, modern education is expressed in a school created by government to which students in many countries are compelled to attend. As most modern schools in Muslim countries are transplanted western institutions, they reflect neither the aspirations nor the necessarily felt needs of the society. They do not for the most part integrate in the community nor help their products to do so. Not surprisingly, in many countries such schools insist on taking the children away from their parents and boarding them in hostels with the result of making the whole system more emphatically artificial and foreign.

2. The Muslim educational institutions place moral and religious training highest on their programme for education *per se* in Islam is religious education. In contrast, many modern educational systems in many Muslim countries have adopted a secular outlook neglecting in the process that most important aspect of education. Consequently the products of this system are alienated from the tradition of their community without having anything in its place. They are left prey to any

new ideas, however untested, illogical or invalid. Without roots in their own tradition, they have nothing with which to measure or evaluate these ideas.

3. Traditional Islamic education was characterized by its lack of rigidity regarding attendance or age grouping. It was possible for a person, regardless of age, to join any class of his choosing and to move on to a higher class once he felt able to cope. As the teaching took place throughout the day from early morning till late into the evening, it was possible for the old to combine education with other responsibilities such as work or family duties. The modern system by its nature precludes such a practice. Admittedly there are evening classes in some institutions in many countries where those who missed education when young can attain it in adulthood. But this is vastly different from the old system in that it is offered in special institutions rather than in the ordinary school.

4. In the Islamic tradition there was no general examination. The student grew into the level of education to which he aspired and his growth was closely watched and evaluated by the teacher. Modern education, though it never tires of deploring the examination system, has failed to find a satisfactory alternative. It is true that continuous assessment has become fashionable in many modern institutions but it has not completely supplanted the old hit-and-miss examination exercise, nor has it fully achieved the fairness and the thorough insight of the traditional system.

5. Traditional higher Islamic education accorded the student a great deal of freedom to choose his own area of interest and to develop his knowledge in that particular area without hindrance. There was no final comprehensive programme for a degree to be attained. Modern education is nothing if not planned minutely and carefully. Such plans might not reflect the reasonable inclination of the student but be an expression of certain prejudices on the part of the planners. An instance of this prejudice is demonstrated by the recently abandoned practice of some British universities in regarding Latin as a prerequisite for reading any university subject whether art, science or technology. Latin was regarded as an essential equipment for the educated gentleman and some even believed it improved the mind.

6. The Muslim educational institutions mirrored the humanity and simplicity of their society. By contrast, the modern school system reflects in some respects Western industrial society. The students are almost treated as if they were objects on a production line. They

110

represent numbers in statistical tables, not persons pursuing the most noble of human endeavours.

7. Islamic educational system was based on the deep personal relationship between the teacher and the taught. The teacher is the source of spiritual as well as professional guidance. Modern educational system is basically impersonal and the function of the teacher is more professional than moral or ethical. Indeed, many a modern teacher considers his professional function to be totally separate from any moral, religious or ethical value. He is a teacher of skills not conduct.

8. Muslim educational institutions were the custodians of the values of the society and the guardians of its heritage. They preserved and safeguarded the culture of the community and where adjustments and change were needed the institutions reflected this need without hurry or pain. The modern school, being an artificial instrument, can lend itself and is often used to change society, sometimes radically and painfully. As an institution working virtually in spiritual and cultural isolation it can act with little concern for the society in which it functions. We are all familiar no doubt with the missionary schools in our countries and with the pernicious influence of the so-called secular schools.

The question that we must now face is whether the modern educational system can be inspired by the aims and purposes of Muslim education; or to put it another way, can the aims and purposes of Muslim education have any value in a modern society? To answer this question we must realize that certain aspects of Muslim education have in the modern age to be abandoned. First, the Muslim states must pursue an interventionist policy. They can no longer stand aside leaving education to the community nor can they fail to enforce education on all their children. They must define the future shape of their society, their economic development using education as the main instrument for preparing the next generation to the projected social organization and economic transformation. Whether we like these aspects that are called progress or not, Muslim societies everywhere are invariably moving towards industrialization and scientific education on a large scale. Indeed, those of them that are lucky enough to have surplus funds are buying more technology than their societies are ready to absorb. Some might argue that Muslims are going the wrong way. But what alternative is there except a return to the pre-scientific age in all its simplicity and the active rejection of modern science and technology? This might have been pleasant if it were possible. Unfortunately, no society can escape the influence of modernity. You either master it or perish by it.[17] Colonialism in its military sense might have receded but in its political and more obviously economic aspects it is still very much with us. The former colonial powers are still the buyers of our raw materials and the suppliers of our manufactured goods. We still pay very heavily for the products of their technology. These products have become the essential tools of our social organization and political administration.

But modernity without moral guidance, religious ethics and the belief in Allah and the destiny of man can bring more unhappiness and cause more disorder and misery. We must bring religion to control the motives of the men of science and guide their conduct in the pursuit of knowledge. This need not hamper scientific advance, on the contrary it should advance it. Let me in this respect quote the words of a scientist: 'Science prospers exactly in proportion as it is religious. . . . The great deeds of philosophers have been less the fruit of their intellect than of the direction of that intellect by an eminently religious tone of mind. Truth has yielded herself rather to their patience, their love, their single-heartedness and their self-denial, than to their logical acumen.' The author of this statement is Professor Huxley, the famous Darwinist, and is quoted with approval by yet another Darwinist, Herbert Spencer.[18]

Science must be self-disciplined. We do not and must not seek to impose from the outside any limit to the activities of scientists or to put constraints on their thoughts since our religion has always emphasized the duty of man to acquire knowledge of the universe and to improve his ability to gain greater benefits from his environment. One need not cite the many verses of the Quran bearing on the subject nor the words of the Prophet (peace be upon him) to the same effect. Our religion, therefore, is not against science but it is against the misuse of science and the misapplication of technology.

Science, it is alleged, can be neutral whereas technology must respond to its environment. It is my contention that science also bears the stamp of its social and intellectual milieu.[19] A society guided by ethical values and the great tradition of Islam can produce a science which is more satisfying to the totality of man. It can produce a technology that is less destructive of man's environment, less motivated by a desire for material benefit and more concerned with the needs and aspirations of a divinely guided community. It is therefore possible, and indeed in the present circumstances imperative, that we should endeavour to establish an educational system based on Islam yet answering all the needs of modern society. It should be noted that currently many western countries are re-examining their educational systems from a very similar point of view. Many people in the West are concerned at the amoral and areligious nature of their schools. They see that often they turn out immoral and irreligious graduates. They see in their society the decline of authority at all levels, the disruption of the family and the lack of social cohesion. They lament the disappearance of the school of the past where ethics and moral values were at the centre of its teaching and organization. What better proof as to the failure of secular education than that its former advocates are now its most vocal critics?

Under a modern Islamic system of education we can look forward to the emergence of a society not dissimilar to that of the Golden Age of Islamic Civilization when all disciplines were thoroughly and fruitfully pursued and where discussion on all aspects of knowledge were freely conducted and where scholars were able to develop their ideas and argue their differences motivated by love of knowledge and a deep sense of piety.

The conflict between science and religion is neither inevitable nor fruitful and in the context of Islam it has no grounds. There is, however, a certain degree of suspicion in Muslim circles as to the impact of western science on Islam. This suspicion is well founded. Western science, it must be remembered, has, for historical reasons, developed in an atmosphere of hostility towards religion and has in the process acquired a negative attitude towards all non-empirical aspects of belief. The basic assumptions of western science are in reality a greater menace to Islamic culture than any hostile work by orientalists.

Modern education is by definition that type of education inspired by the West. It was imposed on our nations sometimes by force of arms and sometimes by enterprising rulers who sought a way of standing up to the West by utilizing the very skills of the West. Generally, the old educational system was retained alongside the new and our people had to endure the divisive, wasteful and illogical system of dual education. When it was decided to come to terms with western education and incorporate it into our system, Western scientific and technological knowledge was accepted fully and almost blindly by us. It has been sufficient to describe a work or a theory as scientific to stifle our critical faculties. Western scientists are looked upon with veneration reminiscent of that conferred by our forefathers on the great founders of the

113

schools of law. By contrast, the contribution of Western philosophers, historians and more especially orientalists has of recent times been critically examined. Indeed, in Muslim educated circles you need only describe a new opinion as emanating from an orientalist source to have it totally condemned. The orientalists and their like are no longer a threat to us. Their open attack can be perceived, examined and countered. But the onslaught of science upon our basic belief and values is indirect and therefore too obscure for the ordinary person or even for the ordinary person or even for the educated to measure and to rebut. Western science assumes the rejection of metaphysics and the meaninglessness of values. In short, it relegates religion to the corner of irrationality and looks upon it with benevolent contempt. Yet science itself is based in the final analysis on irrational assumptions and the fact of its successes should not blind us to this reality.[20]

Our own scientists must involve themselves in the thorough re-examination of science in terms of our culture so as to have it fully assimilated within Islam. Only then will the aims and purposes of Muslim education become meaningful in a modern system of education.

It has been observed that despite the long connection between the Muslim world and the West in the area of scientific studies, the Muslims have so far produced experts but not scientists, technicians but not inventors. This strange and disheartening phenomenon can be explained by the fact that the contradiction between the basis of Western science and the principles of our culture raises a serious conflict which draws our scientists away from full assimilation and participation.

The task of re-examining the basic assumptions of science cannot fall exclusively on the shoulders of the scientists. The scholars of Islam must surely carry part of the burden. They must acquaint themselves fully with the principles of science and the methods of research employed by scientists. Only then will they be able to look into science in terms of our faith and to give an impetus to scientific knowledge and scientific advance in accordance with the dictates and the spirit of our religion. The task I am setting here for our scientists to converge on religion and our religious scholars to converge upon science is not easy. Nor is it a once-and-for-all exercise. It will be a continuous task for which a group of scholars in each generation will have to devote their lives.

We are all familiar with the barrier erected between scientific education and religious education in Muslim countries. The religious scholar is restricted for the most part to the study of his religious discipline without reference in any meaningful terms to modern disciplines and specially to modern science. On the other hand, our scientists are deprived of any meaningful appreciation of our religion and its principles. To be sure, religious lessons have been available in some of our secular or Western-type schools, but they have been superficial, inadequate and completely out of place. On the other hand, some scientific training has existed in some of our religious institutions. But again it has been equally superficial, inadequate and completely out of place. This is not the answer, for it presents not a harmonious relationship between the two types of knowledge but a mere contiguity. We must bring about the Muslim scholar who assimilates science with his religious training. Equally, we must produce scientists who absorb religion with scientific education. The question of assimilation is basic to any programme to find a solution to this problem facing us.

Assimilation is manifested by the total harmony between the various aspects of knowledge and between knowledge and behaviour. Our society needs harmony between knowledge and belief, between science and religion. In the absence of this harmony our scientists may continue to contribute far less than their intellectual gifts warrant. The remedy lies in having knowledgeable piety and pious knowledge. Religion and science must converge and merge within the mind of one and the same individual and within the spirit of the whole community. It is, however, imperative at this point to caution against the practice of some of our scholars who exert a great deal of effort trying to find a correspondence between certain facets of science and certain texts from the Holy Quran or the Prophetic Tradition. While one must appreciate their motives and applaud their intention, one is regretfully compelled to pronounce their efforts as pointless, even harmful. To clarify this point, let me cite one example. Last year an eminent physician published a book on the medical significance of prayer (*salat*). He attributed certain hygienic and curative functions to the body movements which comprise salat and found himself constrained to make a comparison with yoga. It was not difficult for him to show that *salat* was superior to yoga. He expressed it thus: 'Praying exercises are successive graceful movements which represent entire submission to God. They are not mere numbers of physical exercise.'[21] Indeed, they are not. We do not do them for our health but for the worship of our Creator. We follow not the requirements of our body but the dictates of our faith.

Assertions of this kind bring rationalism into an area where human reason should not tread. Our scholars must draw the line between faith and reason, between science and religion. They must learn not to use the tools of the one to research the other. We do not use the ear in the act of seeing nor the eye in the act of hearing. We should equally refrain from employing reason where only revelation must be relied upon. In this respect there is no hostility between revelation and reason any more than there is between the eye and the ear. This demarcation line must express an organic relationship between religion and science at the level of the individual and also in terms of the society as a whole. Clearly, there is tension between the two aspects but this tension is a healthy one for it is a tension that is motivated not by opposition but by co-operation. There is no intention on the part of science to rebel against religion, nor on the part of religion to oppress science. The aim is to define the terms and the areas so that science can function under the aegis of religion. To function as an integral part of the whole act of worship. For in Islam, one of the highest acts of worship is the pursuit of knowledge.

I have so far defined the problem as one between science and religion. I am well aware that science does not comprise the whole of modern education. There is the vast area of the humanities which must be considered by itself. As mentioned earlier, Muslim scholarship was more conscious of the onslaught of western ideas in fields such as philosophy, history and religion. Such ideas have been critically examined and where necessary refuted. However, there is an important point which we must bear in mind, namely that the humanities in the West have succumbed to science. Scientism has become a vogue not only in the study of language but even of literature!

Once we are able to come to terms with science and bring it up to the level of our faith there will be harmony within our society and harmony within our educational system and the place of religious education will have become fully and firmly established within our educational system. We will then be able to heal a world torn by declining standards of faith and value. We can then lead the world to a more harmonious existence when man's power to control his environment is not taken as a rebellion against his Creator and where his religious belief is not regarded as a manifestation of a retarded culture.

But the question is how to bring this happy state about. To begin with, our schools and universities must endeavour to instil the basic principles of our faith into the hearts of their students. The teaching

116

profession should be given back its true function in moral guidance alongside the task of training. The teacher must stand as an example to his students in his observance of the law and his adherence to good behaviour. This is not a plea for a rigid or blind conformity. We recognize the possibility even the necessity of change, but such adjustments must be within the framework of Islam. 'What is *halal* (permissible) is clear and what is *haram* (prohibited) is clear.'[22]

We must, however, guard against the misuse of religion to hamper the innovative spirit of man or to allow its advocates to brandish it as a weapon to stifle any new idea or to cripple scientific enquiry. It is enough for the society to be deeply religious and for the scientist to be so inspired to ensure that he would not step out of line or to misuse science as to impinge on the province of religion. We must also realize that religious knowledge while having the prime place in our educational system, scientific education has to be given its proper place and time. We cannot expect the student involved in learning medicine or engineering or geography or whatever to devote as much time and energy to the deepening of his religious knowledge as those involved in one or other of the specific fields of Islamic studies. The growth of human knowledge necessitates specialization. We must also seek to harmonize religious education with the various disciplines in which the students might be interested. It is true that the principles of Islam and Islamic moral values are immutable but individuals with different background, different interests and different outlooks may view them differently and it is the task of the educator to impart his knowledge in accordance with the need of the student.

Alongside organized institutions, we should return to the old Islamic institutions: the open school for all ages at all levels and needs.

We must endeavour to inject the new institutions with the old fervour for in this way we may very well teach those who are now teaching us technology that though we may be their student in this area of human endeavour we could with justice be their teachers in matters ethical and religious.

Chapter Seven
Transformation of the Perspective

M. Abdul Haq Ansari

Muhammad Abdul Haq Ansari, Reader and Head of the Department of Arabic, Persian and Islamic Studies, Visva Baarati University, West Bengal since 1966, was born in 1931. He got his Ph.D. from Aligarh Muslim University, India in 1962 and M.A. from Harvard University in 1972. His publications include: *The Ethical Philosophy of Miskawaith*; *The Moral Philosophy of al-Farabi*; *The Islamic Ideal*.

Education in an Islamic setting in our age has three dimensions. The first concerns the content of education which consists primarily of ideas, although it also includes work and experimentation. The second concerns the method of education and involves preparation of text books, training of teachers, and building of habits and character on the part of the students. Methods of research in various disciplines may also be mentioned in this context. The third dimension of education is its organization and management. It involves the division of education into lower, middle and higher education and into disciplines and subjects. Instruction in traditional disciplines, such as the study of the Quran, Hadith, and Fiqh, and the education of women and children may be placed in this category.

In this paper we will restrict ourselves to the content of education, particularly the aspect of the content which concerns ideas that constitute particular sciences and disciplines, and ideas that inform the general perspective which shapes the development of particular sciences.

From the point of view of ideas, education at the lower level in an Islamic setting is not a problem. For the ideas that are to be imparted to students at this level may be partly derived from our own traditional resources, and partly taken over from modern text books with little or no modification. The preparation of text books, or the training of teachers for this level are not difficult jobs. They only need faith and determination, and can be carried out at any time.

But at the middle level of education where a student is initiated into various disciplines, the Muslim educationist encounters a real problem which becomes even more serious at the higher level of education. He faces a problem regarding the concepts and theories of particular disciplines as well as the general perspective in which they are worked out. Of course, the nature and gravity of the problem vary according to the discipline concerned. With natural sciences, for instance, the problem is not so much of particular ideas, as of the general view of Nature and the logic of the science concerned. In the case of the social sciences, the problem is not confined only to questions of the general perspective on man and society, but also concerns many of the concepts and theories of these disciplines as they have more or less a direct bearing on the various ideas and ideals of Islam. In philosophical disciplines, which examine knowledge and truth, values and ideals, the conception of God and the world, the nature of man and his destiny, i.e. questions of general perspective, the Muslim educationist faces a problem of great magnitude. He cannot reject part of the modern perspective and accept another. He can select a few ideas, but that would not form a perspective and he must have his own perspective. He must have it spelled out and formulated in such a manner that it can be used in reviewing the literature of various disciplines, before he can write a suitable text book for his students.

During the last hundred years various efforts in the field of education have been made in different parts of the Islamic world, and they have done a great service. But so far as the reorientation of education along Islamic lines is concerned they have only limited success. In traditional madrasas the highest point of achievement is an addition to the curriculum of some European languages and a few modern subjects to give a new look to the teaching of the old subjects. But there has been no modernization of perspective. As a result what we have is a discordant juxtaposition of modern and traditional ideas. On the other hand, in new-styled schools and colleges, the effort in Islamic orientation of education does not go beyond the primary level. What we teach in our institutions at the middle or higher levels is not at all different from what is taught in Western institutions.

The reason is neither the lack of determination, nor the paucity of resources. The reason is the absence of a perspective, which could guide the educationist as well as the scholar and the researcher. What is more deplorable is that many of us are not even conscious of the importance of this perspective; and the proof of this lack of consciousness is that we never plan a concerted effort to work out our own perspective. We do not fully realize that mere talk of Islamic transformation of education,

119

or preparation of text books and training of teachers for middle and higher education is idle before we have a transformation of the perspective.

It is untrue to say we do not have any perspective. We do, but at the level of faith. We do not have it translated in terms of general theory or philosophy which may help us review ideas of modern sciences, and which may guide intellectual pursuits and inspire research. Some may turn for a perspective to that literature which the intellectual leaders of Islamic movements in various countries have brought out during the last fifty years. Remarkable though this literature is in many respects, it is mostly concerned with issues in the practical aspects of social, political and economic fields. Contemporary Islamic thought has so far shown little interest in the issues of general perspective.

One might think that this is an incidental phenomenon but it is not an accident; it has deeper roots in Islamic history and tradition. After the Western domination of the Islamic world in the nineteenth century, Muslim thinking turned away from the outside world and centered on its own problems. As there was no problem of perspective among the Muslims, naturally Islamic thought did not become involved with it. It was diverted to practical problems in society and politics. At the same time, thought in the West was passing through a period of disillusionment with theology and was looking for the essence of religion in moral and social concerns. This trend in Western thought influenced Islamic thinking even further away from the philosophical questions of the perspective. This tendency was welcomed by many sections of Muslim scholars who had always looked on philosophy and theology with suspicion and contempt.

There is another reason why Islamic thought in recent years has been confined largely to social fields. It has been a common belief among Muslim intellectual leaders that the distinction of Islam as a religion lies in its concern with society. Islam is essentially a Sharia. They have been working on the assumption that if the social concern of Islam embodied in the Sharia is sufficiently elaborated in modern idiom, the world at large will be convinced of the truth of Islam, and the *Ummah* will regain confidence in its own future. Muslims will then be urged to struggle for the Islamic transformation of society and for the restoration of Islam's power and glory. This is a common premise of the strategy adopted by the present movements in Islam working for an Islamic revolution. But their experience in the past few years have led many people in these movements to the realization that their under-

120

standing of the problems of the community, particularly the working of the mind of the Western educated ruling class, has been rather superficial. The perspective in which this class looks at things is different from the Islamic perspective which has not been presented to them in recognizable terms. There is a big perspective gap between the ruling class and the Islamic revolutionists. Some in the Islamic movements have also come to ask whether the socio-political approach to Islam in contemporary Islamic literature is sound. They wonder if the stress should not be now placed on the basic questions of the Islamic perspective.

This leads us to ask how Islamic perspective differs from the Western perspective. The major premise of the Western perspective is that all beliefs and ideas, aspirations and institutions which are of their own creation, have developed through a long process of history. Similarly, all perceptions of reality and truth, goodness and beauty are the products of history. There are, of course, various interpretations of the historical process. Some Westerners believe that it is dialectical, some that it is evolutionary, and others have offered their own different formulations. But all of them agree on the human origin and the historicity of all forms of ideas and institutions.

Religion, they believe, is a human creation. If there is reality outside the historical process, as the religious believe, it works in and through history. God or the Divine is immanent in the world. He inspires rather than reveals. Beliefs are human responses and aspirations, and what is called sacred literature is a record of all kinds of fallible human interpretations and experiences sanctified through ritual over a period of history. There is nothing absolute in history, everything is relative and is subject to change and transformation.

A Muslim reader of Western writing on Islam often comes across a ruthless application of the historical method and dismisses it by attributing it to the religious bias of its author. It is, of course, true that most of the earlier works on Islam were produced under a strong religious bias, but many of the recent works are largely inspired by the historical view of knowledge we are talking of. The same view is also applied on a far greater scale to the study of Christianity and there was a time when it was supported by the critics of Christianity. Now, it is used by a growing number of faithful scholars and theologians. As a result we have a vast literature on the history of different books of the Old and New Testaments, on the life of Christ, on the development of Christian beliefs, rituals and worship, values and institutions. The method has also been applied to the study of Judaism, and various other religions, primitive, classical or modern.

Most of the modern literature of Islam by Muslim authors is completely unaware of the historical approach. If it ever goes beyond the boundaries of society and touches the issues of the general perspective the views that it chooses to criticize are the old-fashioned materialism, dilectical historicism, and biological evolution. None of these theories is essential to the historical approach, which is primarily a method, although it has some important philosophical presuppositions. And it is on the account of these presuppositions that the need for the Islamic perspective becomes urgent.

The first problem in the development of an Islamic perspective is the problem of revelation. Contemporary Jewish and Christian theologians understand revelation in the sense of inspiration or the extraordinary quickening of the human spirit, with the clear implication that the content of revelation is essentially human and fallible. They are forced to take this line and interpret the word of God in the Bible in this light because of the modern criticism on the Bible. A Muslim's belief regarding the word of God in the Quran, on the other hand, is that it is a speech articulated by God himself, revealed to the Prophet through an infallible way and preserved in the form that we have it now without the admixture of any element contributed by the Prophet or any other human being. It is in other words meta-historical.

Jewish and Christian writers treat the word of God in the Quran as they treat the word of God in the Bible. They argue their case from two sides. They study the content of the Quran in its historical background, and try to show to their satisfaction that almost all the important Quranic ideas are taken from Christian and Jewish sources, and that the rest are derived from pre-Islamic Arabian society. They also argue from the history of the text of the Quran, as they have constructed it. Literature on the former aspect is quite considerable, on the latter comparatively meagre.

Muslim scholars have looked down on this literature with contempt and refused to take note of it, although it determines the attitude of a great number of men and women in the world and exercises quite a considerable influence on our own educated people. I believe it is high time that Muslims gave up the attitude of ignoring this literature and proceed to subject it to a thorough criticism. Criticism, however, should not be the goal. Rather it should produce a positive account of the history of the Quran text, taking into consideration all the relevant modern research into the origin and development of the Arabic language and script.

Muslims should also make thorough studies on various aspects of the Quran. There are verses in the Quran which refer to natural phenomena, and there are statements on historical events and personalities. There are also remarks on the books of the Jews and Christians – the Torah, the Psalms and the Gospel – and comments on their beliefs and practices. On all these subjects there are numerous observations in commentaries on the Quran and there are also independent works. However, we need fresh efforts on these subjects that take into account modern historical method as well as the critical literature on the Quran and the Bible. Our old literature on the *i'jaz* of the Quran and its divine authorship is outmoded. We have to produce a new literature on the Quranic *i'jaz*.

The second subject that should be taken up with utmost seriousness is research on Islamic values and a comprehensive statement of the entire value system. There is no work on the subject in any Islamic language. There are only a few elementary works on the ethics of the Quran; the other aspects of the system are almost untouched. Traditional literature on Islamic jurisprudence is concerned with the method of finding out the right *hukm* (rule) for a new act or event. With the notable exception of Abū Ishāq al-Shātabī (d. 790/1388) in Spain and Waliy Allah (d. 1176/1762) in India none of the jurisprudents have taken up an investigation into the ends (*maqāsid*) of the Sharia and the relation of the *maqāsid* with *ahkām* (rules and regulations), or to use the terminology of ethics, the relation of the good and the right. Waliy Allāh's work is of a general philosophical nature, whereas Shātabī's work is more factual and analytic. But both studies are far from fulfilling our requirements.

What we need is a comprehensive formulation of the stem structure of Islamic values and its dynamics. We have to know how far various priorities have been actually fixed by the Quran and the Sunnah, and how far they have been left to individuals and societies in various periods and circumstances to define themselves. What is the relation between ends and priorities on the one hand, and changes in technology, industry and population, on the other? We need to know what is *absolute* and what is *relative* in the Islamic values.

Recent works on Islamic society, policy and economy touch on one or the other aspect of Islamic values. They are helpful so far as they go. But in order to have a comprehensive view of the system, one has to investigate the structure and the dynamics of the Sharia as a whole. This is necessary not just for a theoretical understanding of the Islamic values, but also to carry further the work on various aspects of Islamic Society. It is my feeling that the work on Islamic society based upon the jurisprudential principles laid down centuries ago has reached its zenith. A further breakthrough in the work needs a fresh enquiry into the structure of the Sharia and the system of Islamic values.

Another dimension of the work on Islamic values is philosophical. The system has to be viewed in the context of Islamic views on the questions of reality, truth, and the nature of man and his destiny. Without this, the Sharia as a whole or a part of it cannot be fully justified.

The work on Islamic values is also important from the point of view of establishing the rationality of fundamental Islamic beliefs in God and the hereafter. For beliefs in metaphysical truths are to an extent value statements, consequently they are to be justified to that extent in terms of value.

The third problem that I want to mention here concerns the Islamic view of the history of religion. The Quran is interested in the subject in order to show how God has been working in guiding the destinies of the peoples known to the Arabs, and how God acted, and would act, to various responses which people have made or would make to God's message and its bearers. What role various statements of this type have played in the success of the Prophetic mission in Arabia can hardly be over emphasized. Similarly the success of the efforts for Islamic revival in our age will be determined to a considerable extent by the formulation of the Quranic perspective on the history of religion by taking into consideration all that has been made known regarding the religions the Quran mentions and those that it does not.

In this connection it is necessary to point out the differences between an Islamic view of history in general and of the history of religion in particular. The Quran is directly concerned with the latter only. But this does not mean that we cannot have or should not have an Islamic view of history. This is one of the important tasks which scholars should take up. But here I am particularly underlining the work on the history of religion, or the study of the Divine scheme for the guidance of humanity.

There are a number of problems besides those I have mentioned, which are equally important for the development of the Islamic perspective. These concern the nature and the destiny of man, the concept of God, and the place of reason and religious experience vis-a-vis revelation in the formation of a perspective. If I have chosen these three problems or three areas of research for specific mention that is because there is not sufficient realization of their importance and urgency.

Chapter Eight

The Glorious Quran is the Foundation of Islamic Education

Prince Muhammad al-Faisal al-Saud

Prince Muhammad al-Faisal al-Saud, son of King Faisal of Saudi Arabia was educated at Minlo University, California. He worked in various capacities in the government of Saudi Arabia such as the Governor of the Water Desalination Corporation, Jeddah, Director of the Water Desalination Bureau, Expert on Economics at the Saudi Arabian Monetary Agency and Undersecretary of the Ministry of Agriculture and Water. As Founder President of the International Federation of Muslim and Arabic Schools he is doing a great service to Islam by trying to help with the spread of teaching in non-Arabic speaking countries.

Islamic education has its own peculiar character, which distinguishes it very clearly from all other types of educational theory or practice. This distinguishing feature is due to the ambient presence and influence of the Quran on Islamic education. The Quran is, by the consensus of Muslim opinion, in the past and the present, the immutable source of the fundamental tenets of Islam, of its principles, ethics and culture. It is also the perennial foundation for Islamic systems of legislation and of social and economic organization. It is last but not least, the basis of both moral and general education.

This Quranic way has the distinction of connecting all disciplines of the mind with the higher principles of the Islamic creed, morals, social and economic policy as well as with legal practice. The system of Islamic education is based upon the notion that every discipline and branch of knowledge, which is of benefit to society and necessary for it, should be given due attention by the Muslim community or *Ummah* as a whole in order to educate all or some of its members in those disciplines.

Policy of course, depends on the variable needs of society in different times and places. But the presence of highly specialized and deeply learned savants to undertake the task of widening and deepening the scope of knowledge, is a *fardu kifayah* upon all Muslims. This means that all Muslims are in error, or sinful, if they do not designate a few from among themselves recruiting for the study of religion and making themselves truly conversant with the teachings of Islam. To be truly learned in Fiqh *i.e.* general doctrines and the jurisprudence of Islam is not merely to minister to the spiritual but also to the social and wordly needs of the community. But this obligation applies to all disciplines of useful, legitimate and indispensable knowledge. This means that whether this knowledge be of the revelation itself or of any other acquired and purely human knowledge it is obligatory upon some members and therefore upon the community as a whole.

Since the dawn of Islam until this day, many successive generations have been nurtured and taught under the aegis of the Quran. From his tender years the Muslim child begins his education by knowing how to read, then to understand and to commit to memory the holy text. All the other facets of the curricula of that Islamic education are based upon the acknowledgment of the Quran as the core, pivot and gateway of learning.

It was also recognized as the backbone of all disciplines. This Quranic way of education has indeed maintained intact the particularly Islamic personality of the *Ummah* and preserved its basic unity of the thought and culture. As long as the Quran remains the undisputed and immutable pivot of education there is an assured guarantee that the Muslim *Ummah* will keep its integrity and authentic character.

This basic cultural unity is a boon from Allah to Muslims. It is a blessing, the fount of which is this Holy Book. It says: 'If men and Jinn banded together to produce the like of this Quran, they would never produce its like, not though they backed one another.'

This Book is the word of Allah. He has revealed it to the Seal of His Prophets and Quintessence of Messengers as Guidance from Him to mankind and pledged, so to speak, to keep it intact so that it should remain the lighthouse of perennial and continuous Divine guidance for all the successive generations after the Prophet. After the Prophet's death any new revelation which had been the way of knowing the behest from Heaven would never come again, but the Book that had been vouchsafed to Muhammad *Sallallahu alaihi wassalam* was preserved to keep the stream of revelation alive for all time.

(1) Lo! We, even We, reveal the reminder, and Lo! We verily are its guardian.

(2) And thus have We inspired in thee (Muhammad) a spirit of Our command. Thou knewest not what scripture was, nor what was Faith. But We have made it a light whereby We guide whom We will of Our bondmen.

(3) And lo! it is a revelation of the Lord of the Worlds, which the true spirit hath brought down upon thy heart, that thou mayest be of the warners, in plain Arabic speech.

Allah had so willed to honour the tongue of the Arabs by making it the linguistic vehicle for the Holy Book. Thus Allah bestowed upon Arabic the gift of everlasting life to suit the Book, which it had been elected to contain. Allah ordained that Muslims have the Quran committed to memory, recite it and learn its contents.

This comprehension of the Quran cannot be open to people without their being fully conversant with the language in which it has been revealed. Thus it has also become necessary to keep the Arabic language in its original form – in that diction which is of the Quran. Without knowing this conserved Arabic idiom within the Quran, it is well nigh impossible to comprehend the Quran of which every expression is originally linked to what we call classical Arabic.

Since the Muslim community was first illuminated with the right guidance, which is Islam, it has continued to preserve the Quran and keep its language intact in its original form and diction. The results of this fidelity to origins was that the Quran continued to conserve for the Muslim community its authentic character and consequently its pervasive unity of thought and culture, wherein resides its very uniqueness and hence the source of its power.

This unity of thought which had been established by the Quran, always meant, and continues to mean, the capacity for unity, solidarity and co-operation within the fields of knowledge, thought, culture and education.

By this the Muslim community has always transcended the trammels of race, nationality, nationalism and regional considerations. On the contrary, the Muslim community remains the living example of true human unity which is that built on a creed. Humanity is one because its Lord God is one, and its initial ancestor is also one. This concept of the unity of the Muslim community comes out most forcefully in the definition given to it at the Farewell Pilgrimage by the Holy Prophet Himself. He defines this unity in terms of its basis and function.

The Prophet (Sallallahu alaihi wassalam) said: 'No Arab is a better man than a non-Arab; nor is a non-Arab, in any way a better man than an Arab, except by greater fear of God and good works.' This is the proclamation of the quality of all men, which is of the essence of the Islamic ethos.

Thus, since the time of the Message, Islam has abolished all kinds of discrimination whatever the basis. All manner of genetic, ethnic, and nationalistic discrimination was declared inadmissible by Islam; and also the old vainglory about pedigree which had been an accepted mode of social deportment in pre-Islamic Arabia. Yet racial, social or cultural discrimination is one of the more pronounced problems of our time.

The principle of unity of thought, which Islam recommends, is that upon which Islamic education, solidarity and power are built. It is a doctrine of considerable fecundity, of which the root ideas as well as the subsidiary ones impinge upon all kinds of the disciplined quest for knowledge, whether these be of the humanities or the natural sciences or other disciplines of cosmic import.

But the ideological unity, which is derived from the teaching of the Quran, does not end with the unity of the community or the equality of mankind. It also means unity of human knowledge, the relevance of the diverse disciplines whose basic assumptions or general trend of logic tend to contradict each other.

The intellectual unity, epitomized by the Glorious Quran, means the logical unit of the various branches of knowledge and the necessity of effective co-ordination between them, under the guidance of some pervasive wisdom. The source of this unity of human knowledge is the Glorious Book of Allah with its perennial principles and lofty values. As long as the Quran remains a clear and effective means for co-ordination it should suffice to provide the diverse branches of knowledge with principles as well as theological goals. If such a desideratum is achieved, all human disciplines will retain that effective unity which should always yield useful and inspiring knowledge.

Muslims have been wont to go this way from the time of the Message almost to our own day. For all theoretical, practical or religious disciplines were enlightened by this pervasive unity advocated by the Quran. Thus all knowledge became one all-inclusive discipline of which both the spirit and methods were of the Quran.

For that very reason, educational institutions of Islam were public ones that gave Muslim training in and understanding of all the various disciplines which were of relevance to his world and profitable to his society. These were also institutions for specialization after proper general education had been assimilated. Conditions of education followed this pattern until invading armies from the West came to conquer or to impose their alien regimen in direct or indirect ways, in order to exploit the wealth and the labour of Muslim people.

Colonialism and backwardness were both determining factors in introducing aberrations into Muslim educational systems so that they would – as they did – deviate from the age-old Islamic norms. Muslim institutions then ceased to be the vehicles and expressions of a unitary system of education and lapsed after the bifurcation of curricula into cultural ambivalence and educational anarchy.

But Muslim educationists require a master plan and to devise ways and means for achieving a general educational renaissance based upon the foundations of Islam and its well tried perennial curricula. In order to realize such a goal, they will have to begin at the beginning. This means that they should keep to the book that Allah in His mercy has made the foundation of our Islamic tenets of faith, our Islamic juris-prudence and system of laws. This is the Quran which is also the effective guarantee of the cultural unity, the linguistic continuity and the moral integrity of our Muslim Community.

Guidance from the Quran contains no empty slogan. Nor has it the expression of an effete society. It is the nucleus of a complete and integrated programme for education. Suffice it for me to point out the main features of this programme:

The Quran is the same book for all Muslims. In order to maintain its position in the Muslim community we must insist upon unity of pur-pose the faith and cultural integrity. Such unity springs from the Quran; and upon it depends the continued support for the Quran as the fountain head of that unity. But we cannot maintain the cultural unity of Islamic peoples without the thorough unification of educational programmes: in organization, in purpose and in basic structure.

The Quran is there to be understood, taught and consulted as the main guide to action. But it is impossible to reach the desired under-standing of the Quran without prior study of the language in which it has been revealed. To maintain the language of the Quran means spreading knowledge of it, and defending it by bringing it back to its former ascendancy as a universal language; for it is the first tongue of Islam and the reservoir of all the thought, erudition and literature in the cultural heritage of Islam. To preserve the Arabic Language in its authentic form is an absolute necessity if we mean to keep the Quran whole and uncontaminated within admissible interpretations – in other words, fully alive and pregnant with its great legal and moral content.

When Aisha Bint Abubakr spoke of the moral character and deportment of the greatest of Messengers, she gave it in a nutshell by saying that his moral being had been the Quran *i.e.* perfect and exemplary adherence to the precepts of the Quran. We shall maintain the Arabic language, not because it is the national tongue of the Arabs, but because it is the language of the Quran, and therefore the language of Islam.

Learning and education are really holy commitments for all Muslims. Our community is collectively dutybound to give a major part of its attention to education so that a goodly number of members should become versed in all Islamic learning. Allah would take the whole Muslim community to task for extreme negligence if there were insufficient learned men available to serve its people.

The veneration of learning is an age long tradition of Islam. In fact, the quest for learning has always been regarded as an exalted form of worship. It was on account of this sacred regard for learning that mosques, which were and will always be primarily places of worship, were opened for learners and teachers so that these might acquit themselves of their holy duty. Thus for the fourteen centuries of Islam, mosques have remained centres of learning where institutes and even universities were nurtured.

Would to God that Muslims could still hallow their mosques further by restoring to them this ancient and worthy function.

Mosques can still do valuable work in the cultural field, especially in the realm of Islamic authenticity. Such a revival can resuscitate the learned sessions of old and bring back much that might have been lost of our Islamic learning. This revival of the old function of the mosque can go hand in hand with the existence of universities and other independent institutions of learning, whilst aiding them considerably in their important task. If the quest for learning be an obligation, it follows that the taking of measures to have places of learning ready for housing this activity is logically also a necessity. Muslims of all ages and of all classes have always been solicitous of acquitting themselves as groups and individuals of this sacred duty of learning.

History is witness to the fact that Muslims, whether governors or governed were always ready to spend on learning and on the encouragement of savants and 'ulamas. There was always co-operation and mutual emulation in the effective patronization of the learned and in the promotion of learning. This always meant the co-operation of rulers and ruled, of rich and poor towards the maintenance of institutions and the students and teachers working in them. Indeed it never happened throughout our long history as Muslims that individuals or groups relied mainly on government funds.

They were always ready to give generously to institutions of learning. It is only fair to make special mention of the efforts of individuals across the ages in this worthy social endeavour. The great *wakfs* or endowments of the past were not only unstinted and liberal but were most judiciously directed towards the right channels of expenditure when the concern had been education. Muslims continually, through emulation of others and inspiration through Islam, tried to make larger and more efficacious endowments. It is our duty to stir Muslims to better feelings so that they may carry on with the traditions of their forebears in this essential public service of education. Indeed, to promote education to encourage teachers as well as pupils and to found institutions for learning is a sure way of worship and a worthy endeavour to earn the pleasure of Allah and His favour.

It is upon these noble and ancient traditions of Islam that we have created the Foundation of *iman* (*i.e.* of faith) for education and Islamic culture. The purpose of this foundation is to establish modern schools for Islam of the worthiest and most developed standards.

A select group of 'ulama and educationists of considerable reputation and learning have co-operated with us in order to inculcate Islam. We have in fact built a good number of schools in Saudi Arabia, each of which bears the name of *Minaret* in the city of town in which the school has been built.

This nomenclature is meant to symbolize the relationship between schools and mosques within the strong age-old civilization of Islam. We have now a minaret in Riyadh, another in Jeddah and a third in Medina the Radiant. We are now preparing to build a fourth minaret in Cairo. Our object in establishing these schools has been to lay the foundations of a model school for the dissemination of the Arabic culture of Islam and should prove its superior effectiveness in combating irreligious tendencies in national education which have, of late, become prevalent in certain countries.

We have been able to wend our way in a practical and experimental spirit which does not stop at mere things or wise words. This is of course thanks to the intelligent co-operation of parents and guardians and also to the extremely valuable help given to us by some members of the academic staff of Riyadh University, King Abdulaziz University of Jeddah and the University of Imam Muhammad Bin Saud.

In fact, the success of these Iman schools has been found to be greater than expected. Moreover the very existence of such schools is a proof that the culture of Islam is a living and self-renovating culture. This

132

Islamic culture is qualified by its very authenticity and originality to hold its own with the highest and most advanced contemporary cultures.

Few of us can be unaware of the persecution suffered by our institutions, authentic and original education in those Muslim countries which have known the tread of the colonial heel and the grip of foreign imperialist domination.

Colonial administrations used to devise plans for the obliteration of Islamic rules and civilization through the encouragement of secular and atheistic tendencies so that the civilization of Islam should be destroyed. These enemies of Islam also aimed at making more room for missionary societies to do their work.

The effect of this colonialist war which was waged against Islamic institutions is still in evidence in many countries which have gained their political independence. Political independence remains imperfect because the governments of these countries have had neither enough opportunity nor the requisite funds for liberating their systems of education from imperialist domination, culture and language, so as to make their political independence a reality through cultural and educational autonomy.

Despite this imperialistic belligerency, a goodly number of *mujtahidun* are still dauntlessly and with unshaken faith struggling in the field of original education in the Muslim world. We have seen many an heroic example of this type of ideological warrior carry on the sacred battle of Islam in defence of its principles in the field of education.

Appendices

Appendix A: A Select Bibliography

Appendix B: Recommendations of Three Committees

Appendix A

A Select Bibliography

by

S. A. Ashraf

Introduction

It has not been possible for me to trace a comprehensive bibliography on education which will help a scholar to carry out research on all aspects of Islamic education including its aims and objectives. Even Dr. S. H. Nasr's *An Annotated Bibliography of Islamic Sciences* vol. 1 (printed and published in Tehran, 1975) is not altogether comprehensive though it has been a great help in the preparation of this Bibliography. We have the limited objective of helping scholars to find books that will enable them to understand and appreciate the objectives formulated by past thinkers and wise men in the context of Islam and of assisting them to reshape the same objectives in the context of modern life by facing the challenge of dominant alien ideas and thoughts. We have therefore given, first, a list of basic books on Islam and the Islamic concept of man, society and knowledge. In the second section we provide a selected list of books by eminent Muslim scholars who themselves formulated the concepts or whose ideas and thoughts influenced the development of aims and objectives of education in the early Islamic period.

In the third and fourth sections we have tried to give a balanced list of modern writings. The last section comprises a list of those Western writings which were influenced by, or which influenced, Islamic thought on education in the past and of those modern writings and documents which a scholar should study in order to understand the aims and objectives of the modern education that Muslim countries have adopted and find similarities and differences between Islamic and modern thought.

Because of these limited objectives and also because of our intention to initiate research in this field of education these lists have been introduced by some critical comments and an attempt has been made to organize the bibliography according to the Islamic approach to the aims and objectives of education. At a later stage the scholar may or rather will need to prepare a more exhaustive list of writers and their work in different languages. The present bibliography is by no means exhaustive or complete nor does it pretend to give a list of even most of the important works in all the languages of the world or even in European languages. Dr. S. H. Nasr's list of books in European languages given by him in his book *Islamic Science* (World of Islam Festival, London, 1976) overcomes only partially this difficulty. It is necessary for Muslim scholars to prepare a comprehensive bibliography of all such writings in all non-European languages also, especially the languages of the Muslim world.

I. General Background

(1) *Al-Quran* and *Al-Hadith*

Knowledge of Islam and its metaphysics is essential for a scholar who wants to carry out any research into the aims and objectives of education. This knowledge alone provides the basic concepts of Man, his personality, his destiny, the society in which he lives and without which he cannot formulate his objectives. The most important sources for this information are the Quran and the collections of the Hadith of which six are regarded as authentic. There are various interpretations of the Quran (*Tafsir*) of which the most important ones in Arabic, Persian, Urdu and English are recorded below. Some translations and explanations of the *Hadith* collections in different languages are also listed below.

(a) *Al-Quran*

Arabic
(i) *Tafsir* by Tabari, Abu Jafar Muhammad Ibn Jarir (d. 310 H)
(ii) *Tafsir Kabir*: Razi, Fakhruddin Muhammad (d. 606 H)
(iii) *Anwarul Tanzil*: Baidhawi, Qadi Nasiruddin Abu Said (d. 685 H)
(iv) *Tafsir Ibn Kathir*: Ibn Kathir, Abul Fida Ismail (d. 774)
(v) *Tafsir Rahmani*: Shaikh Ali Ibn Ahmed Mahaimi (d. 835 A.A.)
(vi) *Itqan fi ulum-il-Quran*: Suyuti, Jalaluddin (d. 911 H)

(vii) *Tafsir Jalalain*: Suyuti, Jalaluddin and another Jalaluddin.

(viii) *Tafsir*: Abduh, Shaikh Muhammad (d. 1905 A.D.) completed by Muhammad Rashid Rida.

(ix) *Fi Zilal al Quran*: Sayyid Qutb (1906–1966)

Persian and Urdu

Persian: Allama Shamsuddin; Shah Waliullah; Shah Abdul Aziz.

Urdu

Shaikh Abdul Qadir (together with the translation by him)
Maulana Abul Kalam Azad, (*Tarjuman-ul-Quran*) Maulvi Abdul Haqq
(*Tafsir Haqqani*); Maulana Reza Khan Barelivi, (together with the translation); Maulana Shabbir Ahmad Usmani (together with the translation of the *Quran* by Maulana Muhammad Hussain); Maulana Ashraf Ali Thanawi (*Bayanul Quran*); Maulana Muhammad Karam Shah Azhari (*Ziaul-Quran*); Maulana Maududi *Tafhimul quran*); Mufti Muhammad Shafi (*Ma'ariful Quran*).

English

Allama Yusuf Ali, translation and commentary.
Maulana Abdul Majed Dariabadi, translation and commentary. The commentaries by non-Muslims have been excluded because of their perverseness. Similarly the commentary by Muhammad Ali has not been cited because of its serious limitations. Pickthall's *The Meaning of the Glorious Quran* is not a *tafsir*. It is a translation.
For meanings of words and explanations of concepts the following early works should be consulted:
Al-Mufradat: by Abul-Qasim Husain Ragib (d. 503 A.H.)
Al-Kashshaf: Abul-Qasim Mahmud Zamakshari (d. 538 A.H.)

(b) *Al-Hadith*

The six authentic collections in Arabic original (*Sihah Sitta*) are known by the names of the collectors:
Al-Bokhari (194–256 A.H.)
Al-Muslim (204–261 A.H.)
Ibu Majah (209–273 A.H.)
Abu Daud (202–275 A.H.)
Tirmizi (209–279 A.H.)
Nisai (214–303 A.H.)
A new selection from these six and from other collections was made

by Hussain bin Masud al-Fara'd (d. 516 A.H.) Known as *Kitabul Masabih*. This was further improved by Waliuddin Abu Abdullah Muhammad whose edition come to be popularly known as *Mishkat-ul-Masabih*.

Given below are some available translations with commentary in other languages:

Al-Bokhari: Only translation into English with Arabic text by Dr. Muhammad Muhsin Khan published by Hilal Yayinlari Ankara, Turkey.

A translation with a brilliant commentary in Bengali by Maulana Azizul Huq is available now (Hamidia Library, Dacca, Bangladesh).

Sahih Muslim Only the English version with notes and commentary by M. Abdul Hamid Siddiqui, Ashraf, Kashmiri Bazar, Lahore, 1966, rept. 1973.

Mishkat al-Masabih: only the English version by James Robson, Ashraf, Lahore. A version in English and Arabic by Maulana Fazlul Karim, Dacca.

(2) *Prophet's Life*

The next important background material giving material giving the details of organization, structure and system and the practical realization of the aims and objectives of education is available in the biography of Prophet Muhammad (peace and blessings of Allah be on him).

The most notable earliest work in Arabic is *Sira* of Ibn Ishaq (c. 85–151 A.H.) which has been preserved in the recension of Ibn Hisham (d. 218 or 213 A.H.). It has been translated by Professor Von Grünebaun.

Sirat-un-Nabi in Urdu by Allama Shibli Nomani is regarded as an important contribution in this field as yet unsurpassed in scholarship. *Rahmatullil-Alamaan* by Maulana Sulaiman Mansoorpuri (in Urdu) *Mahammad Rasulullah* by Dr. Hamidullah, Centre Cultural Islamic Paris. (French and English)
The life and Teachings of Muhammad or The Spirit of Islam: by S. Ameer Ali (Lahore 1881).

(3) *Islam: basic concepts of Man, Society and knowledge*

(a) The science of Islam is a vast field. For background information the basic works of reference are:

140

The Encyclopaedia of Islam: Leiden: E. J. Brill (1927–   )
Encyclopaedia Britannica (Chapters on Islamic subjects only),
London.

(b) For general and conceptual information the following books
may be consulted:

Corbin, Henry with S. H. Nasr and O. Yahya. *Histoire de la philosophie Islamique*. Paris:
Gallimard, 1964.

Gibb, Hamilton A. R. *Studies in the Civilization of Islam* ed. by S. J. Shaw and W. K. Polk.
Berton: Beacon Press, 1962.

Hamidullah, Dr. M. *Introduction to Islam*. Lahore: Ashraf.

Iqbal, Sir Muhammad. *Reconstruction of Religious Thought in Islam*. Ashraf, 1958.

al-Jili, *De t'homme universal*, transl. by T. Burckhardt. Lyon, 1953.

Nadvi, Abul Hasan Ali. *The Four Pillars of Islam*. Lucknow: Academy.

—— *Western Civilization, Islam and Muslims*. Lucknow: Academy. 1974.

——*Islam and the World*. Lucknow: Academy.

Nasr, S. H. *Ideals and Realities of Islam*. London, 1967.

—— *Science and Civilization in Islam*. Cambridge MSS: Harvard University Press, 1968.

Nasr, S. H. *The Encounter of Man and Nature, the Spiritual Crisis of Modern Man*. London,
1968.

Schuon, F. *Understanding Islam*. London, 1961.

—— *Dimensions of Islam*. London, 1970.

——*Islam and the Perennial Philosophy*. World of Islam Festival Publishing Co., London,
1976.

Sharif, M. M. *A History of Muslim Philosophy* (ed.). 2 vols: Wiesbaden: O. Harrasswitz,
1963.

Shustery, Muhammad Abbas. *Outlines of Islamic Culture*. 2 vols. Bangalore, 1938.

(c) Other books and Articles for further consultation (including
books by some Orientalists).

Alwaye, A. M. M. 'The Conception of Human Responsibility in Islam' in *Majilla't al
Azhar*. pp. 4–7, Oct, 1969.

Aqqad, Abbas Mahmud al. *Al Insan Fi'l Quran al Karim* (Arabic Text) being *The Concept
of Man in the Quran*. Cairo: Dar al Hilal, 1960.

Arberry, A. J. *The Koran Interpreted*. 2 vols. London/New York: George Allen and
Unwin, 1955.

——*Revelation and Reason in Islam*. London: George Allen and Unwin, 1957.

——*Aspects of Islamic Civilization as Depicted in the Original Texts*. London: George Allen
and Unwin, 1964.

Boer, de T. J. trans. Jones, E. K. *The History of Philosophy in Islam*. London: Luzac,
1903.

Cragg, Kenneth, *The Privilege of Man. A Theme in Judaism, Islam and Christianity*. London:
The University of London Athlone Press, 1968.

—— *The House of Islam*. California: Dickenson Publishing Inc. Belmont, 1969.

——*The Event of the Quran: Islam in its Scriptures*. London: George Allen and Unwin,
1971.

———*The Mind of the Quran: Chapters in Reflection.* London: George Allen and Unwin, 1973.

Cobb, Stanwood *Islamic Contributions to Civilization.* Washington. D.C.: Avion Press, 1963.

Elder, E. E. 'The Conception of University in early Islam' in *Muslim World*, 17, pp. 11–30, 1927.

Fadel, Aly Omar: 'Estimation of mankind in Islam', in *Majillat al Azhar* (*Journal of Al-Azhar*, pp. 9–12, Nov. 1966.)

Gibb, Dr. Hamilton. *Mohammadanism*, Oxford.

Gilani, Sayid Munazir Ahsan. *Nizam i Ta'leem O Tarbiyat.* 2 vols. (Urdu Text) being an account of the Muslim Educational system in India from 1200 A.D. to the present day. Hyderabad, India: Usmania University Press, 1943.

Goitein, S. D. *Studies in Islamic History and Institutions.* E. J. Brill, Leiden, 1968.

Grünebaum. G. E. Von. *Unity and Variety in Muslim Civilization.* University of Chicago, Chicago/London, 1955.

——— 'Islam in a Humanistic Education', *Journal of General Education*, 4. pp. 12–31, 1949.

——— *Islam: Essays in the Nature of Growth of a Cultural Tradition*, Routledge and Kegan Paul: London, 1961.

———*Problems of Muslim Nationalism in Social Change.* The Colonial Situation (ed.) J. Wallestein, John Wiley, New York, 1966.

Hamid, Khawaja A. 'The Body versus Soul Fallacy in the Quran', in *Islamic Culture* 14. pp. 423–429, 1940.

———'The Conception of Man in Islam' in Islamic Culture, 19. pp. 133–66, London 1945.

Hunter, W. W. *The Indian Mussalmans*, Calcutta, 1945.

Huq, S. Moimal. *The Great Revolution of 1857*, Karachi, 1968.

Khan, Sayyid Ahmed (Sir Syed Ahmad Khan) *Majallat-i-Sir Sayyid Ahmed Khan*, Collected by Maulana Ismail Panipati (in Urdu), Lahore, n.d.

Malik, Charles, *God and Man in Contemporary Islamic Thought*-Proceedings of the Philosophy Symposium held at the American University of Beirut, February 6–10 Beirut, 1972.

Masumi, S. H. 'The Concept of Society in Islam' in *Journal of the Pakistan Philosophical Society.* Vol. VII No. IV pp. 42–50, 1963.

Qureshi, I. H. *The Muslim Community of the Indo-Pakistan Sub-Continent.* The Hague, 1961.

Rohman, S. *An Introduction to Islamic Philosophy.* Mallick Bross, Dacca, 1956.

Sarwar, Alhaj G. *Philosophy of the Quran.* Ashraf: Lahore, 1965.

Smith, H. B. 'The Muslim Doctrine of Man': Its bearing on social policy and Political Theory, in *Muslim World* 44. pp. 202–48, 1954.

II. Early Muslim Thinkers

GENERAL

Arnaldez, R., and L. Massignon, 'La science arabe' in R. Taton (ed.). *La Science antique et médiévale (des origines à 1450)*, vol. I of the editor's series *Histoire générale des sciences*, Paris, 1957; English translation by A. Pomerons as *Ancient and Medieval Science*, New York, 1963, and London, 1965.

Browne, E. G. *Arabian Medicine*. Cambridge, 1921.

Browne, E. G. *A Literary History of Persia*. 4 vols. London, 1902–24.

Burckhardt, T. *Alchemy*, transl. by W. Stoddart. Olten, 1960.

Burckhardt, T. *Fes, Stadt des Islam*. Olten, 1960.

Burckhardt, T. *Moorish Culture in Spain*, transl. by A. Jaffa. London, 1972.

Corbin, H., S. H. Nasr, and O. Yahya, *Histoire de la philosophie islamique*, vol. I. Paris, 1964.

Duhem, P. *Le système du monde: histoire des doctrines cosmologiques de Platon à Copernic*, 10 vols. Paris, 1913–59; especially vols. II and IV.

Dunlop, D. M. *Arabic Science in the West*. Karachi, 1958.

Elgood, C., *A Medical History of Persia and the Eastern Caliphate*. Cambridge, 1951.

Eliade, M. *The Forge and the Crucible*, transl. by S. Corrin. New York, 1962.

Encyclopaedia of Islam, 1st edition, London and Leiden, 1908–38; new edition, Leiden and London, 1960 on.

Miéli, A. *La science arabe et son rôle dans l'évolution scientifique mondiale*. Leiden, 1938, 2nd ed. Leiden, 1966.

Nasr, S. H. *An Annotated Bibliography of Islamic Science*, vol. I. Tehran, 1975.

Nasr, S. H. *Islamic Science*. World of Islam Festival, 1976.

O'Leary, De L. *How Greek Science Passed to the Arabs*. London, 1964.

Peters, F. E. *Allah's Commonwealth*. New York, 1973.

Peters, F. E. *Aristotle and the Arabs, the Aristotelian Tradition in Islam*. New York and London, 1968.

Sarton, G. *Introduction to the History of Science*, 3 vols. Baltimore, 1927–48.

Walzer, R. *Greek into Arabic*. Oxford, 1962.

Wolfson, H. A. *Crescas' Critique of Aristotle: Problems of Aristotle's Physics in Jewish and Arabic Philosophy*. Cambridge (U.S.A.), 1929.

AL-KINDI d. 873 A.D.

Kitab aqsàm al-ilm al-insa (The classification of Human Sciences).

Risâlat al-Kindî fî ḥudûd al-ashyâ' wa-rusûmihâ in *Rasâ'il* 163–79.

Rasâ'il al-Kindî al-falsafiyya, ed. Muḥammad 'Abd al-Hâdî Abû Rîda (Cairo 1369/1950).

Atiyeh, G. N. *Al-Kindi, the philosopher of the Arabs*, Rawalpindi, 1966.

AL-FARABI d. 950 A.D.

Falsafat aflâṭun (De Platonis philosophia), ed. F. Rosenthal and R. Walzer ['Corpus Platonicum Medii Aevi, Plato Arabus', v. 2] (Londinii 1943).

Maqâla fî ma'ânî al-'aql (Der Intellect), in *Rasâ'il* 39–48.

Iḥṣâ' al-'ulûm (La statistique des sciences), ed. Osman Amine (2nd ed.; Cairo 1949).

Risâla fî mâ yanbaghî an yuqaddam qabl ta'allum al-falsafa (Die Vorstudien zur Philosophie), in *Rasâ'il* 49–55.

Risâla fî faḍîlat al-'ulûm wa-l-ṣinâ'ât (2d ed.; Hayderabad 1367/1948).

Haymond, Robert. *The Philosphy of Al-Farubi and its influence on medieval Thought.* New York, 1947.

Mahdi, Mulhsin. *Al-Farabi's Book of Religion.* Beirut, 1963.

IBN SINA (AVICENNA) d. 1037 A.D.

Fî al-ajrâm al-'ulawiyya, in Tis' rasâ'il 39–59.

Fî aqsâm al-'ulûm al-'aqliyya, in *Tis' rasâ'il* 104–119.

Fî al-qiwâ al-insâniyya wa-idrâkâtihâ, in *Tis' rasâ'il* 60–70.

al-Shifâ'. MS Leiden, No. 1445. Numbers indicate the part, section, sub-section, and chapter *(jumla, fann, maqâla, faṣl).* Cf. M.–M. Anawati *Mu'allafât Ibn Sînâ* (Essai de bibliographie Avicinnienne) (Cairo 1950) 30 ff., 76: 14–15.

Tis' rasâ'il fî al-ḥikma wa-l-ṭabî'iyyât (Cairo 1326/1908).

Avicenna Commemoration Volume, Iran Society, Calcutta, 1956.

Morewedge, P. (tr.) *The Metaphysics of Avicenna.* London 1973.

Gruner, O. C. *A treatise on the Canon of Medicine of Avicenna, Incorporating a Translation of the First Book.* London, 1930.

Afnan, S. M. *Aviccuna, his Life and Works.* London, 1958.

Nasr, S. H. *An Introduction to Islamic Cosmological Doctrines.* Cambridge, Mass., 1964 (pp. 177–274).

Nasr, S. H. *Science and Civilization in Islam,* pp. 29–49, 62–112.

Nasr, S. H. *Three Muslim Sages,* pp. 9–52.

IBN RUSHD (AVERROES) d. 1198 A.D.

Faṣl al-maqâl wa-taqrîr mâ bayn al-sharî'a wa-l-ḥikma min al-ittiṣâl (Traité décisif sur l'accord de la religion et de la philosophie), ed. L. Gauthier ['Bibliothèque arabe-française', ı] (3rd ed.; Alger 1948).

Kitâb jâmi' mâ ba'd al-ṭabî'a (Compendio de Metafisica), ed. C. Rodríguez (Madrid 1919).

Kitâb al-kashf 'an manâhij al-adilla fî 'aqâ'id al-milla wa-ta'rîf mâ waqa'a fîhâ bi-ḥasab al-ta'wîl min al-shubah al-muzîgha wa-l-bida' al-muḍilla, in *Thalâth rasâ'il* 27–128.

Kitâb al-nafs (Hayderabad 1366/1947).

Tahâfut al-tahâfut (transl. by S. van den Bergh Gibb Memorial Series 19), London, 1954.

Thalâth rasâ'il (Philosophie und Theologie), ed. M. J. Müller ['Königlich-Bayerische Akademie der Wissenschaften: Monumenta Saecularia', I. Classe [No.] 3.] (München 1859).

Tafsîr mâ ba'd al-ṭabî'a (Grand Commentaire de la Metaphysique d'Aristote), ed. M. Bouyges ['Bibliotheca arabica scholasticorum, série arabe', t. V–VII] (3 vols.; Beirut 1938–48).

Talkhîṣ kitâb al-nafs (Paraphrase du 'De anima'), ed. A. el-Ahwanî. Cairo, 1950.

On the Harmony of Religion and Philosophy tr. George F. Hourani. London, 1961, rept. 1967.

Gauthier, L. *Ibn Rochd* (Averroes). Paris, 1948.

Renan, E. *Averroes et Averroisme.* Paris, 1952.

IBN MISKAWAYHI d. 1030 A.D.

Tahzib al-Akhlaq. Beirut, 1961.

AL-BIRUNI d. 1048 A.D.

The Book of Instruction in the Elements of the Art of Astrology, transl. by R. R. Wright. London, 1934.

Al-Bīrūnī Commemoration Volume. Calcutta, 1951.

Al-Bīrūnī's India, trans. with a preface by C. E. Sachau, 2 vols. London, 1888.

IKHWAN AL-SAFA (fl ca. 100 A.D.)

Rasâ'il Ikhwân al-Safâ' wa-khillân al-wafâ', ed. Khayr al-Din al-Zarkalî. Cairo, 1347/1928.

Dispute between Man and the Animals. Trans. by J. Platts. London: W. H. Allen and Co., 1869.

AL-GHAZZALI d. 1111 A.D.

Ihyâ' 'ulûm al-dîn (15 vols.; Cairo 1356/[1937]–1357/[1938]).

The Book of Knowledge (Bk 11 of Ihya, tr. by Dr. Nabih Amin Faris, Ashraf, Lahore, 1962.

Tahâfut al-falâsifa (Incohérence des Philosophes), ed. M. Bouyges ['Bibliotheca arabica scholasticorum, série arabe', t. II] (Beirut, 1927).

Kitâb al-Maḍnûn al-ṣaghîr. On the margin of 'Abd al-Karîm Ibn Ibrâhîm al-Jîlânî al-Insân al-kâmil fî ma'rifat al-awâkhir wa-l-awâ'il II (1368/1949) 89–98.

O Youth tr. of Ayyuha'l-walad by G. H. Scherer, Beirut, 1933.

The Confessions of Al Ghazzai, tr. by C. Field, London, 1909

Gardner, W. R. W. An account of Ghazzali's Life and Works. Madras, 1919.

Jabre, F. la notion de la certitude selon Ghazali. Paris, 1958.

Jabre, F. la notion de Marifah chez Ghazali. Paris, 1958.

Smith, Margaret Al-Ghazali, the Mystic. London, 1944.

Watt, W. M. The faith and practice of al-Ghazali. London, 1953.

Watt, W. M. Muslim Intellectual: A study of Ghazali. Chicago-Edinburgh, 1963.

Wensink, A. J. La Pensée de Ghazzali. Paris, 1940.

Zwemer, S. M. A Moslem Seeker After God. New York, 1920.

IBN BAJJA (AVEMPACE) d. 1138 A.D.

Tadbîr al-mutawaḥḥid (El régimen del solitario), ed. M. Asín Palacios. Madrid, 1946; another ed. Beirut, 1978.

Opera Metaphysica ed. Majid Fakhry, Dar al-Mahl. Beirut, 1968.

AL-RAZI, FAKHRUDDIN d. 1029 A.D.

Kitâb muḥaṣṣal afkâr al-mutaqaddimîn wa-l-muta'akhkhirîn min al-falâsifa wa-l-mutakallimîn. Cairo, 1323 A.H.

al-Mabâḥith al-mashriqiyya, 4 vols. Hyderabad, 1924–25.

145

NASIRUDDIN AL-TUSI (d. 1274 A.D.)

Majmua al-Rasail, 2 vols. Hyderabad: Deccan, 1939–1940.
Akhlaq – i – Nasiri tr. by G. M. Wickens. London, 1964.

IBN KHALDUN, ABD AL-RAHMAN (1332–1406 A.D.)

The Muqaddimah, tr. into English by F. Rosenthal 3 vols. New York: Pantheon
Books, 1958.
Inan (Enan), M. A., *Ibn Khaldun, his life and work*, trans. from Arabic (Ibn
Khaldun: *hayātuhu wa turāthuhu al-fikri*, Cairo, 1933). Lahore, 1944.
Mahdi, Muhsin, *Ibn Khaldun's philosophy of History*. London: Allen & Unwin, 1957.
Nasr, S. H., *Science and civilization in Islam*, 56–7, 62–66, 230.
Schmidt N. *Ibn Khaldun, historian, sociologist and philosopher*. New York, 1930.

MULLA SADRA (d. 1642)

Asfar al-Arba'a. Tehran, 1865.
Rahman, Fazlur, *The Philosophy of Mulla Sadra*. Albany, 1975.

III. Education: Books on Muslim education by modern scholars

Ahmed, M. *Muslim education and the scholars' social status up to the 5th century Muslim Era* 11th
century Christian Era) in the light of Ta'rikh Baghdad. Zurich, 1968.
Baloch, N. A. *Nahj al-Ta'allum*. A mid-sixteenth century work on education. Sind Univ.
Research J. Arta Series, 1962, 2:47–60.
Dodge, R. *Muslim education in medieval times*. Washington, 1962.
Gibb, H. A. R. *The university in the Arab-Muslim world*, 1939.
Goldziher, I. 'Education (Muslim)'. *Encyclopaedia of religion and ethics*, 5:198:207.
Haskins, C. H. *The rise of universities*. New York, 1923, 143 pp.
Husain, Zakir. *Educational Reconstruction in India*. Delhi, 1958.
Law, N. N. *Promotion of learning in India during Muhammadan rule, by Muhammadens*.
London, 1916, 308 pp.
Keddie Nikki R. *Scholars, Saints and Sufis- Muslim Religious Institutions in the Middle East
since 950 A.D.* University of California, Berkeley/Los Angeles/London, 1972.
—— *Sayyid Jamal-al-din Al-Afghani*. A Political Biography. Berkeley/Los Angeles/
London: University of California Press, 1972.
Maududi. Sayed Abu'l Ala. *Mutalaba-i-Nizam i Islami*: speech delivered in Urdu on the
Demand for the Islamic System of society in Pakistan (Urdu Text). Lahore:
Jamat-i-Islami Publications, 1948.
—— *Naya Nizam i Ta'leem* (Urdu Text) on Modern Muslim Education address deli-
vered at Dar al Ulum at Nadwa on Jan 5, 1941. Lahore, 1957.

146

—— *Islami Nizam i Ta'leem* (Urdu Text) on the Muslim Education: suggestions for Pakistan, speech delivered at the Barket Ali Muhammad Hall, Lahore, 1952. Lahore: Jamat-i-Islami Publications.

——*Ta'aleemat*: (Urdu Text) A collection of Maulana's views on Muslim Education. Lahore: Jamat-i-Islami Publications, 1947.

Mujeeb, M. *Education and Traditional Values*. Meerut, 1905.

Nadvi, Syed Abul Hasan Ali. *Nahwe al Tarbiyatal-Islamiat el Hurra fi hakumat wa-al-balad-al-Islamiyya* (in Arabic). Al-Mukhtar -al-Islami, Cairo, 1976.

Nadvi, S. Suleman. *Islami Nizam-i-Ta'leem* (Urdu Text) on Muslim Educational System. Darul Musannifin, Azamgarh, 1938.

Nakosteen, M. *History of Islamic Origins of Western Education A.D. 800–1350*. With an introduction to medieval Muslim education. Boulder (Colorado), 1964.

Nasr, S. H. *Science and Civilization in Islam*. Cambridge, 1968.

Nuseibeh, Hazem Zeki, *The Ideas of Arab Nationalism*. Ithaca, New York: Cornell University Press, 1959.

Qubain, F. I. *Education and Sciences in the Arab World*. Baltimore, 1966.

Quraishi, Mansoor Ahmad. *Some Aspects of Muslim Education*. Centre of *Advanced Study in Education*. Faculty of Education, M. S. University of Baroda, India, 1970.

Qureshi, I. H. *Education in Pakistan*. Maaref Ltd: Karachi, 1975.

Rahman, Fazlur. *New Education in the making in Pakistan*. London, 1953.

Rosenthal, Franz. *Knowledge Triumphant: The Concept of knowledge in Medieval Islam*. E. J. Brill: Leiden, 1970.

Saqeb, G. N. *Modernization of Muslim Education*. London, 1977.

Sayili, A. *The institutions of science and learning in the Moslem world* (dissertation), Cambridge (Mass.), 1942.

Shalaby, A. *History of Muslim Education*. Beirut, 1954.

Talas, A. *L'enseignement chez les Arabes-La Madrasa Nizamiyya et son histoire*. Thesis Paris, 1939.

Tibawi, A. L. *Islamic Education: its Traditions and Modernization into the Arab National Systems*. London, 1972.

Totah, K. A. *The contribution of the Arabs to education*. New York, 1926.

Tritton, A. S. *Materials on Muslim Education in the Middle Ages*. London, 1957.

Waheed A. *The Evolution of Muslim Education.*: A Historical Psychological and Cultural Study of the influences which have shaped Muslim Education. Islamic College Peshawar/Feraze & Sons: Lahore, 1945.

Wustenfeld, F. *Die Akademien der Araber und ihre Lehrer*. Göttingen, 1837; Neudruck, 1970.

al-Zarnuji. *Tal'lim al-muta'allim-Tariq al-ta'allum*. Instruction of the student: the method of learning, trans. by G. E. von Grunebaum and T. M. Abel. New York, 1947, 83 pp.

147

IV. Education: Articles on Muslim education, past and present by modern scholars.

Abdul Mu id Khan, M. 'The Muslim theories of education during the middle Ages'. *IC*, 1944, 18: 418–33.

Abdulwahab, H. H. 'Bayt al-Hikma ou 'Mason de la Sagesse' d'lfriqiya'. *IBLA*, 1965, 28: 353–72.

Ahmad, N. 'Progress of education, knowledge and science under the Muslim rule of the world'. Islamic literature, 1956. B(Mar.): 37–42.

Alwaye, A. M. M. (1965) 'The Quran and the Freedom of Belief' in *Mujillat al Azhar*. (Journal of Al-Azhar University) P. 12 (March 1965) 'The Effects of the Belief in the Oneness of God', in *Majillat al Azhar*, pp 3–4.
  (Sept. 1968) 'The Role of Islam in the Spread of Knowledge,' in *Majilla't Al Azhar*, pp. 3–4, 13.

Bastide, H. dela. 'Les universities islamiques d'Indonesie'. *Orient*, 1962, 21: 81–4.

Bausani, A. 'L'odierno ordinamento degli studi islamici nella' madrasa' Mir-i Arab di Bukhara. *Oriente Modermo*, 1954, 34:395–404.

Berque, J. 'Ville et universite.' Aperçu sur l'histoire de l'école de Fès', *Revue de L'hist. du droit franc. et étranger*, 1949, 27: 64–117.

Bowen, H. 'The Nizamiya Madrasa and Baghdad topography'. *JRAS*, 1928: 609–14.

Brunschwig, R. 'Quelques remarques historiques sur les medersas de Tunisie'. *Revue Tunisienne*, 1931:261–85.

Buchanan, J. R. 'Moslem schools in Syria'. *Trans. of the Glasgow oriental soc.*, 1913–22, 4:51–5.

Buchanan, J. R., 'Moslem education in Syria (Before the war)'. *MW*, 1922, 12: 394–406.

Contini, F. 'Storia delle istituzioni scholastiche dell Libia', 1953, 1(3): 5–101.

Dar, M. I. 'Al-Ghazzali on the problem of education'. *Shafi presentation vol.*, 1955: 33–40.

Donaldson, D. M. 'The shrine colleges of Meshed'. *MW*, 1926, 16:72–8.

Doolittle, M. 'Muslim' religious education in Syria'. *MW*, 1928, 18:374–80.

Draz, M. A. 'Al-Azhar'. *Int. social sci, bull.* 1953, 5: 698–701.

Eberman, V. A. 'Meditsinskaya shkola v Dzhundishapure (L'ecole de médecine de Gundisapur)'. *Zapiski Kollegii Vostokovedov*, 1925, 1:47–72.

Elgood, C. 'Jundi-Shapur. A Sassanian university'. *Proc. of the Royal soc. of med.*, 1939, 32: 1033.

Gaulmier, J. 'Note sur l'etat present de l'enseignement traditionnel a Alep'. BEO, 1942, 9:1–33.

Grünebaum, G. E. von, and Abel, T. M. 'The contribution of a medieval Arab scholar to the problem of learning'. J. of personality, 1946–7, 15:59–69.

Hamidullah, M. (1939), 'Educational System in the time of the Prophet'. *Islamic Culture*, 13. pp. 48–90.
  (1970) 'The Islamic Conception of Life'. *Majillat al Azhar*, 42. i. pp. 10–16, 42, iv. pp. 5–8, 42. v. pp. 9–13.

Hussain, S. M. 'Islamic education in Bengal'. *IC*, 1934, 8: 439–47.

Jaffar, S. M. 'Islamic education'. *Shafi presentation vol.*, 1955:119–129.

Jamali, F. 'The theological colleges of Najaf'. *MW*, 1960, 50:15–22.

Khan, M. A. M. 'The Muslim theories of education during the Middle Ages'. *IC*, 1944, 18:418:33

Khan, Y. H. 'The educational system in medieval India'. *IC*, 1956, 30:106–25.

Khudabukhsh. 'The educational system of the Muslims in the Middle Ages'. *IC*, 1927, 1:442–72.

Kissling, H. J. 'Die saziologische und padagogische Rolle der Derwischorden im osmanischen Relche'. *ZDMG*, 1953, 103:18–28.

Lecomte, G. and Canard, M. 'Sur la vie scolaire a Byzance et dans l'Islam'. *Arabica*, 1954, 1:324–36.

Lelong, M. 'L'enseignement superieur Islamique'. *IBLA*, 1962, 25:181–4.

Louis, A. 'Sujets d'examen proposés aux etudiants de la Grande Mosquée'. *IBLA*, 1953, 16:247–54.

Majerczak, J. 'Notes sur l'enseignement dans la Russie Musulmane avant la revolution'. *Revue du monde musulman*, 1917–18, 34:179–246.

Makdisi, G. 'Muslim institutions of learning in eleventh century Baghdad'. *BSOAS*, 1961, 24:1–56.

Martinovitch, N. N. 'Turkish education in the eighteenth century'. *MW*, 1930, 20:37–44.

Marty, P. 'Le College Musulam Moulay Idris'. *Renseignements Coloniaux*, 1925:1–16.

Marty, P. 'L'Universite de Qaraouiyne'. *Renseignements coloniaux*, 1924:329–53.

Mathur, V. B. 'Muslim education in India (1765–1928)'. *Studies in Islam*, 1967, 4:125–62; also, *IC*, 1967, 41: 173–83.

Michaux-Bellaire, E. 'L'enseignement Indigene au Maroc'. *Revue du monde musulman*, 1911, 15:422–52.

Moussa, M. Y. 'Avicenne et I'Azhar'. *Revue du Caire*, 1951, 27(141):140–65.

Muchrif, al-. 'La réforme de l'enseignement à la grande mosquée de Tunis'. *REI*, 1930, 4:441–515.

Nasr, S. H. 'The immutable principles of Islam and Western education'. *Iqbal Review*, 1966, 7 (3):82–7; also *MW*, 1916, 6:189:94.

Pedersen, J. 'Some aspects of the history of the Madrassa'. *IC*, 1929, 3:525–37.

Pérétié, A. 'Las Madrasas de Fès'. *Archives Marocaines*, 1912, 18:257–372.

Pickthall, M. 'Muslim education'. *IC*, 1927, 1:100–8.

Podgorny, G. 'Islamic-Persian medical education, a survey from Jundi-Shapur to Cairo'. *North Carolina med. J.*, 1966, 27:135–40, 203–8.

'Le programme des etudes chez les chiites et principalement chez ceux de Nedjef, Par un Mesopotamien'. *Revue du monde musulman*, 1913, 23:268–79.

Putney, E. W. 'Moslem philosophy of education'. *MW*, 1916, 6:189:94.

Quraishi, M. A. 'The educational ideas of Ibn Khaldun'. *J. of the Maharaja Sayajirao univ. of Baroda*, 1965, 14: 83–92.

Quraishi, M. A. 'Al-Ghazzali's philosophy of education'. *J. of the Maharaja Sayajirao univ. of Baroda*, 1964, 13(1):63–9.

Quraishi, M. A. 'A glimpse of Muslim education and learning in Gujarat'. *J. of the Maharaja Sayajirao univ. of Baroda*, 1968, 17:45–56.

Quraishi, M. A. 'Muslim teachers and students (in the middle Ages)'. *J. of the Maharaja Sayajirao univ. of Baroda*, 1967. 16(1):21:38.

Renaud, H. P. J. 'L'Enseignement des sciences exactes et l'édition d'ouvrages scientifiques au Maroc avant l'occupation européenne'. *Archeion*, 1931, 13: 325–36; also in *Hesperis*, 1932, 14: 78–89.

Renon, A. 'L'éducation des enfants des le premier age, par l'Imam Al-Ghāzāli, texte et traduction'. *IBLA*, 1954, 8:57–74.

Ribera y Tarrago, J. La ensenansa entre loa musulmanes espanoles. Bibliofilos y bibliotecas en laEspana musulmana. Tercera edicion. Cordoba, 1925.

Ribera y Tarrago, J. 'Origendel Colegio Nidami de Bagdad'. *Homenaje a D. Francisco Codera*, 1904: 3–17: also in the same author's *Disertaciones y opusculos*, 1928, 1:361–83.

Rosenthal, F. 'The Techniques and Approach of Muslim Scholarship'. *Analecta Orinetalie*. Roma, 1947.

Rossi, E. 'L'istituzione scolastica militare "al-Futuwwah" nell'Iraq'. *Oriente moderno*, 1940, 20:297–302.

Sadiq I. 'Avicenna on education'. *Indo-Iranica*, 1956, 9(4):71–7.

Shaltout. M. (1960) 'Islam, the Religion of Mind and Knowledge' in *Majilla't al Azhar*, 32 pp 4.11.

Sanial, S. C. 'The Itimad-ud-daulah institution at Delhi'. *IC*, 1930 4:310–23.

Sanial, S. C. 'History of the Calcutta Madrassa'. *Bengal past and present*, 1914, 8:83–111, 225–50.

Sayili, A. 'Gondishapur'. *EI* 2:1120.

Sayili, A. 'Higher education in Medieval Islam. The Madrasa'. *Annales de l'Universite d'Ankara*, 1947–8, 2:30–69.

Sekaly, A. 'L'Universite d'El Azhar et ses transformations'. *REI*, 1927, 1:95–116, 465–529; 1928, 2:47–165, 255–337, 401–71.

Semaan, K. 'Education in Islam, from the Jahiliyyah to Ibn Khaldun'. *MW*, 1966, 56:188–98.

Slassi, A. A. 'L'Universite de Gand-I Shahpur et l'étendue de son rayonnement'. *Melanges H. Massé*, 1963:366–74.

Siddiqi, B. H. 'Ibn Miskawaih's theory of education'. *Iqbal*, 1962, 11:39–46.

Snider, N. 'Mosque education in Afghanistan'. *MW*, 1968, 58:24–35.

Sourdei, D. 'Les professeurs de Madrassa à Alep aux XIIᵉ – XIIIᵉ siècles d'apres Ibn Saddad'. *BEO*, 1949–51, 13:85–115.

Tawfiq, M. A. 'A sketch of the idea of education in Islam'. *IC*, 1943, 17:317–27.

Tibawi, A. L. 'The idea of guidance in Islam from an educational point of view'. *IQ*, 1956, 3:139–56.

Tibawi, A. L. 'Muslim education in the Golden Age of the Caliphate'. *IC*, 1954, 28:418:38.

Tibawi, A. L. 'Origin and character of *al-madrasah*'. *BSOAS*, 1962, 25:225:38.

Tibawi, A. L. 'Some educational terms in Rasa'il Ihwan as-Safa'. Int. Congr. of orientalists, XXIV, 1957: 297–9. Also *IQ*, 1959, 5:55–60.

Titus, M. T. 'A study in Moslem religious education'. *MW*, 1936, 26:385–8.

Tritton, A. S. 'Arab theories of education', *J. of Indian hist.*, 1925, 3(3) and 4(1):35–41.

Tritton, A. S. 'Muslim education in the Middle Ages (circa 600–800 A. H.)' *MW*, 1953, 43:82–94.

Vollers, K. 'Azhar'. *EI*, 1:532–9.

Waardenburg, J. 'Some institutional aspects of Muslim higher education and their relation to Islam'. *Numen*, 1965, 12:96–138.

V. Aims of Education in the West: for Comparison

GENERAL

Barclay, W. *Educational Ideals in the Ancient World*. Collins, 1959.
Beck, F. A. G. *Greek Education 450–350 B.C.* Methuen, 1964.
Boyd, W. *The History of Western Education*. A. & C. Black, revised edition 1964.
Bronowski, J. and B. Mazlish, *The Western Intellectual Tradition*. Pelican, 1963.
Browning, O. *A History of Educational Theories*. Kegan Paul, 1914.
Brubacher, John S. *Modern Philosophies of Education*. New York: McGraw-Hill Book Company, Inc., 1939.
Brubacher, John S. (editor), *Philosophies of Education*. The Forty-Yearbook of the National Society for the Study of Education. Part I. Bloomington, III.: Public School Publishing Company, 1942.
Curtis, S. J. *An Introduction to the Philosophy of Education*. University Tutorial Press, 1958.
Curtis, S. J. and M. E. A. Boultwood. *A short History of Educational Ideas*. University Tutorial Press, 1961.
Educational Policies Commission, *The Purposes of Education in American Democracy*. Washington, D. C.: National Education Association, 1938.
Horne, Herman Harrell. *The Democratic Philosophy of Education*. New York: The Macmillan Company, 1932.
Horne, Herman Harrell. *The Philosophy of Christian Education*. New York: Fleming H. Revell Company, 1937.
Rusk, R. R. *Doctrines of the Great Educators*. Macmillan, 1954, revised ed. 1965.
Rusk, R. R. *The Philosophical Bases of Education*. University of London Press Ltd, 1928.
Ulich, R. *History of Educational Thought*. American Book Co., 1945.
Welton, J. *What Do we mean by Education?* Macmillan, 1915.

Ancient Thinkers

PLATO

Adamson, J. E. *The Theory of Education in Plato's Republic*. Swan Sonnenschein, 1903.
Bluck, R. S. *Plato's Life and Thought*. Routledge and Kegan Paul, 1949.
Bosanquet, B. *The Education of the Young in the Republic of Plato*. Cambridge University Press, 1917.
Boyd, W. *Plato's Republic for Today*. Heinemann, 1962. (selected and transl. with an educational commentary)
Burnet, J. *Greek Philosophy – Thales to Plato*. Macmillan, 1914.
Crossman, R. H. S. *Plato Today*. Allen and Unwin, 1937.
Dickinson, G. L. *Plato and His Dialogues*. Pelican, 1947.
Kitto, H. D. F. *The Greeks*. Pelican, 1951.
Lodge, R. C. *Plato's Theory of Education*. Routledge and Kegan Paul, 1947.
Nettleship, R. L. *Lectures on the Republic of Plato*. Macmillan, 1898.

151

—— *The Theory of Education in Plato's Republic*. Oxford University Press, 1938.

Plato, *The Dialogues*. Translated by B. Jowett. Four volumes. New York; Charles Scribner's Sons, 1872, 4th revised ed. Oxford, 1964.

ARISTOTLE

Allan, J. D. *The Philosophy of Aristotle*. New York: Oxford University Press, 1952.

Barker, E. *The Political Thought of Plato and Aristotle*. New York: Putnam, 1906.

Burnet, J. *Aristotle on Education*. Cambridge University Press, 1903.

Davidson, T. *Aristotle and Ancient Educational Ideals*. Heinemann, 1892.

Muirhead, J. H. *Chapters from Aristotle's Ethics*. Murray, 1900.

Ross, W. D. *Aristotle*. Methuen, 1923.

QUINTILIAN

Colson, F. H. *Quintiliani Institutio Oratoria*. Cambridge University Press, 1924.

Gwynn, A. *Roman Education from Cicero to Quintilian*. Oxford University Press, 1926.

Hodgson, G. *Primitive Christian Education*. T. Clark: Edinburgh, 1906.

Smail, W. H. *Quintilian on Education*. Oxford Univiersity Press, 1938.

Wilkins, A. *Roman Education*. Cambridge University Press, 1921.

ST AUGUSTINE

Fr D'Arcy, M. C. *The Philosophy of St Augustine*. Sheed and Ward, 1934.

Augustine, St. Aurelius. *Treatise on the city of God*. Two volumes. Edited by Marcus Dods. Edinburgh: T. & T. Clark, 1871.

Oates, W. J. (ed.). *Basic Writings of St Augustine*. New York: Random House, 1947.

Papini, G. *St Augustine*. Hodder and Stoughton, 1930.

ST THOMAS AQUINAS

Copleston, F. C. *Aquinas*. Pelican, 1955.

Mayer, M. H. *The Philosophy of Teaching of St Thomas Aquinas*. Milwaukee: Bruce Publishing Co, 1928.

Pegis, A. C. (ed.). *The Basic Writings of Aquinas*, 2 vols. New York: Random House, 1945.

ERASMUS

Born, K. L. (ed.). *The Education of a Christian Prince, by Erasmus*. Columbia University Press, 1936.

Bouyer, L. *Erasmus and the Humanist Experiment*. Chapman and Hall, 1959.

Huizinga, J. *Erasmus of Rotterdam*. Phaidon Press, 1952.

Hyma, A. *Erasmus and the Humanists*. New York: Appleton-Century-Crofts, 1930.

Smith, P. *Erasmus*. Harper and Row (New York), 1923.

Woodward, W. H. *Studies in Education during the Age of the Renaissance 1400–1600* (ch. 4, Erasmus). Cambridge University Press, 1906.

Zweig, S. *Erasmus of Rotterdam*. New York: Viking Press, 1934.

LUTHER

Maritain, J. *Three Reformers: Luther, Descartes and Rousseau*. Sheed and Ward, 1928.

Painter, F. V. N. *Luther on Education*. Philadelphia: Lutheran Publishing Soc., 1890.

COMENIUS

Keatinge, M. W. *The Great Didactic of John Amos Comenius*, 2 vols. A. & C. Black, 1896.
Monroe, W. S. *Comenius and the Beginnings of Educational Reform*. Heinemann, 1900.
Piaget, J. (ed.). *John Amos Comenius*. UNESCO, 1957.
Sadler, J. E. *J. A. Comenius and the Concept of Universal Education*. Allen and Unwin, 1966.
Spinka, M. *John Amos Comenius*. Chicago University Press, 1943.
Turnbull, G. H. *Hartlib, Drury and Comenius*. Liverpool University Press, 1947.
Young, R. F. *Comenius in England*. Oxford University Press, 1932.

Modern Thinkers

DESCARTES

Descartes, Rene. *Discourse on Method*. Translated by John Veitch, La Salle, III. The Open Court Publishing Company, 1945.

MILTON

Ainsworth, O. M. *Milton on Education*. Yale University Press, 1928.
Clark, D. L. *John Milton at St Paul's School*. A Study.

LOCKE

Locke, John. *Some Thoughts Concerning Education*. With Introduction and Notes by R. H. Quick, Cambridge, England: At the University Press, 1934.

HOBBES

Hobbes, Thomas. *The English Works of Thomas Hobbes*. Collected and edited Sir William Molesworth, Bart. Ten volumes. London: John Bohn, 1889.

FROEBEL

Froebel, F. *Autobiography*. Swann Sonnenschein, 1899.
Hughes, J. L. *Froebel's Educational Laws for all Teachers*. Arnold, 1910.
Kilpatrick, W. H. *Froebel's Kindergarten Principles Critically Examined*. New York: Macmillan, 1916.
Lawrence, E. *Friedrich Froebel and English Education*. University of London Press Ltd., 1952.
Froebel, F. W. A. *The Education of Man*. Translated and annotated by W. N. Hailman. New York: D. Appleton & Company, 1899.

ROUSSEAU

Rousseau, Jean Jacques. *Emile*, London: J. M. Dent and Sons, Ltd., 1943.
Rousseau, Jean Jacques. *Social Contract*. In Sir Earnest Barker, *Social Contract: Essays by Locke, Hume, and Rousseau*. New York/Oxford University Press, 1948.

KANT

Horne, Herman Harrell. 'An Idealistic Philosophy of Education'. Bloomington, III:
   Public School Publishing Company, 1942.
Kant, Immanuel. *The Critique of Pure Reason*. Translated by J. M. D. Meiklejohn.
   Revised edition: London and New York: The Colonial Press, 1900.
Kant, Immanuel. *Fundamental Principles of the Metaphysics of Ethics*. Translated by Otton
   Manthey-Zorn. New York: D. Appleton-Century Company, 1938.
Kant, Immanuel. *The Critique of Practical Reason*. Translated by L. W. Beck, Chicago:
   University of Chicago Press, 1949.
Annette Churton. *Kant on Education*. Kegan Paul, Trench, Trubner, 1889.

JOHN STUART MILL

Anschutz, R. P. *The Philosophy of the John Stuart Mill*. Oxford University Press, 1953.
Britton, K. *John Stuart Mill*. Penguin, 1953.
Cavenagh, F. A. *James and John Stuart Mill on Education*. Cambridge University Press,
   1931.

SPENCER

Spencer, Herbert. *First Principles of a New System of Philosophy*. Second edition; New York:
   D. Appleton & Company, 1896.
Spencer, Herbert. *Education: Intellectual, Moral, and Physical*. New York: D. Appleton &
   Company, 1889.

HUXLEY

Huxley, Thomas Henry. *Science and Education*. New York: D. Appleton & Company,
   1896.

DEWEY

Dewey, John. *Democracy and Education*. New York: The Macmillan Company, 1916.
Dewey, John. *Reconstruction in Philosophy*. London: University of London Press, Ltd.,
   1921.
Dewey, John. *Human Nature and Conduct*. New York: Henry Hold and Company, 1922.
Dewey, John. *Experience and Nature*. Chicago: The Open Court Publishing Company,
   1925.
Dewey, John. *Experience and Education*. New York: The Macmillan Company, 1938.
Brickman, W. W. (ed.). *John Dewey: Master Educator*. National Society For Advance-
   ment of Education, 1959.
Childs, J. L. *American Pragmatism and Education, An Interpretation and Criticism*. New York:
   Henry Holt, 1956.
Dworkin, M. S. *Dewey on Education*. Columbia University Press, 1959.
Geiger, G M. *John Dewey in Perspective*. Oxford University Press, 1958.
Handlin, O. *John Dewey's Challenge to Education*. New York: Harper and Row, 1959.
Hollins, T. H. B. 'The Problem of Values and John Dewey' in *Aims in Education: The
   Philosophic Approach*. Manchester University Press, 1964.
Horne, H. H. *The Democratic Philosophy of Education*. New York: Macmillan, 1932.
Mayhew, K. C. and A. C. Edwards. *The Dewey School*. New York: Appleton-Century-
   Crofts, 1936.

Ratner, J. *The Philosophy of John Dewey*. Allen and Unwin, 1928.
Schlipp, P. A. *The Philosophy of John Dewey*. New York: Tudor Publishing Co., 1939.

WHITEHEAD

Schlipp, P. A. *The Philosophy of Alfred North Whitehead*. New York: Tudor Publishing Co., 1951.
Whitehead, A. N. *Science and the Modern World*. Cambridge University Press, 1927.
Whitehead, A. N. *Aims of Education and other Essays*. London, 1929.
Hartshorne, C. (ed.). *Whitehead's Philosophy selected Essays 1935–70*. London, 1972.

PERCY NUNN

Tibble, J. W. 'Percy Nunn 1870–1944' in *British Journal of Educational Studies*. Vol. X No. I Nov. 1961.
Sir Percy Nunn. *Education: Its Data and First Principles*. Third edition, E. Arnold, 1945.

BERTRAND RUSSELL

Park, J. *Bertrand Russell on Education*. Allen and Unwin, 1964.
Russell, Bertrand. *Education and the Special Order*. London, 1930.
Russell, Bertrand. *On Education, especially in early childhood*. London, 1926.

OTHER MODERN WRITINGS ON AIMS OF EDUCATION

Adams, J. *The Evolution of Educational Theory*. Macmillan, 1915.
Archambault, R. D. (ed.). *Philosophical Analysis and Education*. Routledge and Kegan Paul, 1965.
Bagley, W. C. *Education and Emergent Man*. Ronald, 1934.
Barzum, J. *The House of Intellect*. Secker and Warburg, 1959.
Brubacher, John S. *Modern Philosophies of Education*. Second edition. New York: McGraw-Hill Book Company, Inc., 1950.
Brubacher, John S. (editor). *Eclectic Philosophy of Education*. New York: Prentice Hall, Inc., 1951.
Childs, John L. *Education and the Philosophy of Experimentalism*. New York: Century Company, 1931.
Childs, John L. *Education and Morals: An Experimentalist Philosophy of Education*. New York: Appleton-Century-Crofts, Inc., 1950.
Castle, E. B. *Moral Education in Christian Times*. Allen and Unwin, 1958.
Coe, G. A. *A Social Theory of Religious Education*. Scribner, New York, 1917.
Conant, J. B. *The Citadel of Learning*. Yale University Press, 1956.
Durkheim, E. *Moral Education*. Free Press of Glencoe, 1961.
Eliot, T. S. *Notes Towards a Definition of Culture*. Faber, 1959.
Eliot, T. S. *To Criticize the critic and other writings*. Faber: London, 1965.
Griswold, A. W. *Liberal Education and the Democratic Ideal*. Yale University Press, 1959.
Harvard University's Committee on General Education. *General Education in a Free Society*. Harvard U. P. 1945.
Hollins, T. H. B. (ed.). *Aims in Education, the Philosophic Approach*. Manchester University Press, 1964.
Hughes, A. G. and Hughes, E. H. *Education: Some Fundamental Problems*. Longmans, 1960.

Jeffreys, M. C. V. *Education: Christian or Pagan*. University of London Press Ltd., 1946.

Jeffreys, M. C. V. *Glaucon, An Inquiry into the Aims of Education*. Pitman, 1950.

Livingstone, R. W. *Education and the Spirit of the Age*. Oxford University Press, 1952.

McGucken, William J. *The Catholic Way in Education*. Milwaukee: The Bruce Publishing Company, 1934.

Mannheim, K. *Diagnosis of our Time*. Routledge and Kegan Paul, 1943.

Maritain, J. *Education at the Crossroads*. Yale University Press, 1943.

Niblett, W. R. *Christian Education in a Secular Society*. Oxford University, Press, 1960.

Peters, R. S. *The Concept of Education*. Routledge & Kegan Paul, New York: The Humanities Press, 1970.

Peters, R. S. *Ethics and Education*. Allen & Unwin, 1966.

Dearden, R. F., Hirst, P. H., and Peters, R. S. (eds). *Education and the Development of Reason*. Routledge & Kegan Paul, 1972.

Appendix B

Recommendations of Committees 1, 3 & 4

Committee 1

Definition and Aims of Education

Chairman: Dr. Syed Muhammad Al-Naquib Al-Attas

Preamble

No definition of education, no clarification of its aim is possible unless the nature of man and the significance of knowledge are first made clear.

Man according to Islam is composed of soul and body, the soul rational and the body animal; he is at once spirit and matter; he is a unity as an individual and his individuality is referred to as the self; he is endowed with attributes bestowed by Allah. Man possesses spiritual and rational organs of cognition such as the heart (قلب) and the intellect (عقل), and faculties relating to physical, intellectual and spiritual vision, experience and conciousness. He is forgetful by nature and inclines towards injustice and ignorance. His most important gift is knowledge which pertains to spiritual as well as intelligible and tangible realities. Knowledge must guide him towards a high ultimate destiny in the Hereafter, which is determined by how he conducts himself in this world.

Islam is a special body of knowledge granted to man by God, Who is the source of all knowledge. Knowledge is a trust (أمانة) which must be borne with responsibility and justice and wisdom with reference to man and nature (طبيعة). In nature are found signs of knowledge which must be approached in reverential humility and with purity of purpose.

Definition of Education

The meaning of education in its totality in the context of Islam is inherent in the connotations of the terms Tarbiyyah (تربية), Ta'lim (تعليم), and Ta'dib (تأديب) taken together. What each of these terms

157

conveys concerning man and his society and environment in relation to God is related to the others, and together they represent the scope of education in Islam, both 'formal' and 'non-formal'.

Aims of Education

Considering that Islam offers Man a complete code of life in the Quran and the Sunnah which, followed wholeheartedly, leads Man towards the realization of the greatest glory that Allah has reserved for him as Khalifatullah;

considering also that in order to follow the code of Islam adequately and attain to a consciousness of himself as Khalifatullah Man needs training from his childhood, both at home and in the society in which he lives, and that this training should be of his total personality, his spirit, intellect, and rational self, imagination and bodily senses, and not of one part at the expense of others;

considering further that his faith in the code and practice according to this faith are possible only when the training is so organized that all other aspects of his personality are dominated by his Spiritual self which alone can receive and strengthen faith, develop his will-power and lead Man to good deeds and salvation;

considering also that the Western classification of knowledge underlying the modern system of education prevalent in Muslim countries is based on a secular concept which ignores the necessity of faith as the basis of action as required by Islam and which considers whatever training of feelings, imagination and reason Natural Sciences, Social Sciences and Humanities can give as sufficient for the growth of human personality;

considering finally, that in view of the fact that, though all Muslim countries teach Islam as one of the many subjects they have not as yet substituted Islamic concepts for anti-Islamic concepts, it is imperative to reclassify knowledge and reorganize education;

it is hereby resolved that:

1. Education should aim at the balanced growth of the total personality of Man through the training of Man's spirit, intellect, rational self, feelings and bodily senses. The training imparted to a Muslim must be such that faith is infused into the whole of his personality and creates in him an emotional attachment to Islam and enables him to follow the Quran and the Sunnah and be governed by the Islamic system of values willingly and joyfully so that he may proceed to the realization of his

status as Khalifatullah to whom Allah has promised the authority of the universe;

2. Planning for education be based on the classification of knowledge into two categories:

a. 'Perennial' knowledge derived from the Quran and the Sunnah meaning all Sharia-orientated knowledge relevant and related to them, and

b. 'Acquired' knowledge susceptible of quantitative and qualitative growth and multiplication, limited variations and cross-cultural borrowings as long as consistency with the Sharia as the source of values is maintained;

3. Education by precept and example should instil piety and encourage self-purification as a means of penetrating the deep mysteries of the universe and opening the heart to the fear and love of Allah;

4. Education should promote in man the creative impulse to rule himself and the universe as a true servant of Allah not by opposing and coming into conflict with Nature but by understanding its laws and harnessing its forces for the growth of a personality that is in harmony with it;

5. There must be a core knowledge, which must be made obligatory for all Muslims at all levels of the educational system from the highest to the lowest, graduated to conform to the standards of each level;

6. The core knowledge at the university level, which must first be formulated before that at any other level, must be composed of ingredients pertaining to the nature of man (انسان); the nature of religion (دين) and man's involvement in it; of knowledge (معرفة وعلم)and wisdom (حكمة) and justice (عدل) with respect to man and his religion; the nature of right action (أدب وعمل). These will have to be referred to the concept of God, His Essence and Atributes (توحيد), the Revelation (القرآن) its meaning and message; the Revealed Law (الشر) and what necessarily follows: The Prophet, his life and Sunnah, and the history and message of the Prophets before him; the arkan (أركان الاسلام) the religious sciences (علوم الشريعة.) and knowledge of Islamic ethics and moral principles and *adab*, the knowledge of the Arabic language and of the Islamic world view as a whole;

7. That an Islamic University be established in line with the above resolutions;

8. That a body of experts be gathered to formulate the details of the core knowledge as well as the knowledge of sciences;

9. Basic necessary knowledge must be imparted to all Muslims. To

159

attain this aim, basic primary education must be provided for all children and illiteracy eliminated from the Muslim world;

10. Contemporary knowledge in the field of scientific and social development and information must be given to pupils at all levels;

11. The Educational system in the Muslim world must be shaped so as to facilitate social mobility. All barriers must be removed to give equal opportunity to all Muslims to attain to the highest stages in society according to their capacities.

Committee 3

Islamic Education in the Past and its Present Heritage

Chairman: Shaikh Abul Hasan Ali Nadwi
Co-chairman: Dr. Abdullah bin Abul Mohsin al-Turki

The third Committee of Group 'A' arrived at the following recommendations:

1. The Character of education at all stages, in all areas of knowledge, should be Islamic so as to enable students to comprehend and meet challenges to their faith.

2. The aim of this type of education, should be to preserve the Islamic heritage and to resist the encroachment of alien cultures.

3. 'Kattatib' schools should be made the foundation of primary schooling, and they should be provided with necessary facilities to do their work.

4. Muslim governments, organizations and individuals should use their moral influence and provide material assistance to strengthen the foundation of 'Kattatib' education in countries with Muslim minorities. The Conference recommends the setting up of a special committee to plan and supervise the implementation of this recommendation.

5. Muslim countries should establish Islamic institutes designed to produce capable teachers of Sharia and Arabic subjects in the primary, preparatory and secondary stages, and to undertake the formulation of unified programme based on Islam in combination with other branches of knowledge.

6. Opportunities should be afforded to graduates of Basic Studies

Institutes to work in the various fields of life according to their specialization, through material and moral inducements.

7. The Arab countries should reinforce the teaching of the Arabic language materially and morally in the non-Arabic speaking Islamic countries, and should strive to make it a basic language in these countries, and assist the efforts exerted by the people of those countries towards that end.

8. The memorizing and understanding of suitable portions of the Holy Quran and Hadith should be made compulsory at all stages of education.

9. The Committee recommends the establishment of Islamic universities which should teach modern sciences in addition to religious subjects. Studies in these universities should be diversified so that the graduates of each department should master both the Sharia and one of the other subjects and thus constitute a generation of scholars qualified in modern subjects each in his own field.

10. An Islamic Research Academy staffed by scientific and technical experts, and supplied with adequate equipment and financial support should be established to authenticate, edit and publish Islamic manuscripts.

11. Ministers of Education in Muslim countries should take an active interest in student circles and unions all over the world, with a view to involving them in Islamic activities and providing them with material and moral support against hostile and subversive currents.

Committee 4

Education Policy and Practice

Chairman: Dr. Kamel Baqir
Co-chairman: Dr. Taher Abdur Razek

Having reviewed educational systems prevailing in the world, namely the European, American and Marxist systems in addition to mixtures of such systems, and considered the traditional systems in some Muslim countries, the committee believes that it is high time to formulate an alternative Muslim educational system to be adopted in Muslim countries, which will be designed to serve as a defence against ideological and behavioural deviation resulting from intellectual and ethical on-slaughts.

The committee maintains that educational policy in the Islamic countries should emphasize the creation of good men believing in God who are earnest in their pursuit of this life and the life hereafter in accordance with Quranic injunctions.

1. A Muslim educational system must articulate Islam's perception of the individual, society and the physical cosmos in its relation to the Creator, Allah, the Almighty.
2. The fundamentals of such a system should combine the following:
   a. Promotion of Faith from the nursery and primary level to university education.
   b. Islamic teachings and laws which mould the individual's social education, namely, the Articles of the Faith.
   c. Islamic teachings relating to al-Muamlat (social intercourse);
   d. such Islamic ethical rules of conduct which seek to build man's morals, namely, al-Tahzeeb (Refinement).
3. The Committee believes the Holy Quran, the Hadith, the example set by the Prophet's life and the scientific and cultural achievements of the early Muslims should form the spring-board for the proposed educational system.
4. The Committee believes that such a system should encourage due respect to reason and intellect, promote the study of science and harness it to the good of mankind.
5. The Committee maintains that educational policy should seek to promote the formulation of Islamic theories in the fields of economics, politics, sociology and philosophy in order to fill the vaccuum in the minds of Muslim youth in these areas, so as to prevent intellectual invasion from outside.
6. The Committe believes that a Muslim educational system should emphasize Islam's respect for freedom combined with its emphasis on discipline and social order.
7. Education could not be Islamic either in planning or execution unless the community and the state adopt the Islamic system. There-fore, all countries in which Muslims form a majority are urged to abide by the Shariah and make their economic, political and social legislation in accordance with Islam relying on the Quran and the Hadith.
8. The educational system should be so designed that all social and

162

natural sciences as well as arts should have an Islamic core. Developments in these areas should be accelerated qualitatively and quantitatively within the Islamic frame of reference.

9. The Committee believes, that once the suggested Islamic system has been set up the dualism existing in educational systems in some Islamic countries should be reconsidered. The Committee, however, warns against abolishing traditional Islamic institutions before working out a substitute that would preserve the Islamic legacy.

10. The Committee believes that universities in Muslim countries could embark on the training of scientists and technicians who would pioneer social and economic development. Such universities should have an Islamic frame of reference and would, for instance, try to turn out Muslim medical doctors, Muslim engineers, Muslim agronomists . . . etc.

11. To realize the aforementioned aim, the Sharia faculties should occupy a pivotal role in the structure of universities. All other disciplines, including engineering and agronomy should be closely related to them.

12. Considering that the Sharia faculties have a limited influence on other faculties because of the influence of anti-Islamic concepts on students through direct or indirect 'brainwashing' a Committee of select Muslim scholars should be commissioned to initiate research in all disciplines. Their findings should be completed within a period of five years with a view to working out a clear perception of Muslim concepts which should provide basic guidance. Such fields of research should include:

   a. Developing and simplifying the Islamic Juridical system within the framework of Sharia.

   b. Creating an economic system guided by Sharia and avoiding usurious interest rates.

   c. Principles of criticism in the field of literature, arts, crafts and fine arts.

13. A Centre for Theoretical and Applied Research be established whose activities would be primarily concerned with Islam and its relation to social, applied, philosophical and intellectual sciences; the development and reform of education plans for different stages.

14. The Committee is of the view that the teacher is an effective force in the implementation of the proposed system and it, therefore, emphasizes that the proposed education policy will not bear fruit unless the policy, plans and curricula of Education Colleges in the universities

163

and teacher training institutes are revised with an eye to the teacher's creed, behaviour, and professional and vocational training.

15. The Committee recommends that a provisional body be immediately set up with Muslim thinkers and educationists participating in this Conference – renowned for their knowledge, experience and sincerity – to study existing education systems and draw up guide lines for an Islamic system of education.

16. The Committee deems it necessary to establish a permanent World Council for Islamic Education, supported by the Islamic countries, to study educational Problems, in the light of Islamic aims and concepts.

17. The Committee is of the view that immediate steps must be taken as soon as practicable to implement the proposed system at the four levels of education, from the kindergarten to the university, in a gradual and integrated manner.

18. The Committee deems it urgent that a wide publicity campaign be launched to define this system and to highlight the shortcomings of the imported system.

19. The Committee is of the view that the proposed Islamic system of education should ensure the segregation of the sexes at all stages of education, and not permit any kind of co-education.

20. The Committe considers that the initiation of the proposed Islamic system entails the following:

    a. to secure the approval of the governments concerned.

    b. to begin immediately the preparation of teachers along new lines, as well as to organize in-service training sessions for present teachers.

    c. to prepare curricula for text books.

21. The Committee recommends the establishment of a World Islamic Organization for Education, Culture and Science at Islamic government level – for the consolidation and development of Islamic education and give special care to Islamic culture and civilization.

22. Education of Muslim Minorities:

22.1 Intensive and continuous action must be undertaken to persuade Muslim parents of the necessity of providing basic Islamic learning for all Muslim boys and girls.

22.2 It is necessary to draw up uniform curricula for basic Islamic education in the Islamic maktabs and schools that are run solely by Muslim communities.

22.3 Wherever the general policy bans religious teaching in state institutions, the Muslim community can apply for a permit for this type

164

of education by giving an assurance that its finances will be met by the Muslim community and that it will be extra-curricula.

22.4 The lessons taught in the Muslim maktabs and schools must be designed in a manner allowing students multiple entry points to state institutions.

22.5 Measures must be taken to train teachers to teach basic Islamic education by modern methods.

22.6 Text books suitable for basic Islamic education must be published in all important languages employed by Muslim minorities.

22.7 The Islamic countries must reserve places in their specialized colleges and technical institutes for students from Muslim minority countries.

Notes

Introduction

1. See Conference Book, First World Conference on Muslim Education, King Abdulaziz University, Jeddah-Mecca, 1393 A.H. – 1977 A.D., 'Recommendations', p. 78,1;1.1.
 2. Ibid., pp. 88–89.
 3. In fact *ibadah* in its entirety is but another expression of *adab* towards God.

Religion, Knowledge and Education

I. Preliminary Thoughts on the Nature of Knowledge and the Definition and Aims of Education

1. For an expository account of the concept of *din* and other related concepts, see Syed Muhammad al-Naquib al-Attas: *Islam : the concept of religion and the foundation of ethics and morality*, Kuala Lumpur, 1976. The present paper is based on the above work, and a more comprehensive perspective of the subject discussed herein can be better envisaged by consulting the work.
 2. For a summary of the various ideas on knowledge expressed by Muslim thinkers covering the above periods, se al-Tahanawi: *Kashshaf estilahat al-funun*, the article on *'ilm*. Most of it is derived from data contained in the *al-Muwaqif* of Adud al-Din al-lji, who made extensive use of Al-Amidi's *Abkar al-Afkar*.
 3. There have been many attempts made by Muslim thinkers to define knowledge philosophically and epistemologically, the best definition – according to al-Amidi in his work cited in Note 2 and also in another work – the *Ihkam fi usul al-ahkam* – was that made by Fakhr al-Din al-Razi. Ibn Hazm, and also al-Ghazali in his *Maqasid al-Falasifah*, have distinguished the meaning of definition as being of two types, one referring to a description of the nature of the object defined (*rasm*); and the other to a concise specification of the distinctive characteristic of the object defined (*hadd*). We are here, however, not concerned with a philosophical or epistemological definition of knowledge, but more with its general classification designed to be applied to a system of order and discipline in the educational system.

IV. The Islamic as Opposed to Modern Philosophy of Education

1. Quaran: II, 269.
 2. Perhaps it is not accidental, that in modern industrial societies the word wisdom, and other terms such as selflessness and chastity, which from the traditional point of

view are meaningful in education, have either been transformed into archaic words; or if they are used, they are preceeded by the word 'old'.

3. S. H. Nasr defines the term intellect ('aql) from the Islamic point of view, as follows '. . . in Islamic philosophy, the term ('aql) embraces both the rational and the intellectual which stands above the domain of reason.'
Report on the joint Session of the Institute International de Philosophie and the Imperial Iranian Academy of Philosophy, in: *Sophia Perennis*, vol. I, no. 2, supplement no. 1.
September 1975, Tehran, p. 10. See also, S. H. Nasr: *Sufi Essays*, London, 1972, chapter on 'Revelation, Intellect Reason in the Quran', pp. 52–56.

4. Frithjof Schuon: *Logic and Transcendence*, trans. by P. N. Townsend, New York/ Evanston/San Francisco/London, 1975, pp. 7–18.

5. R. S. Peters: 'Must educators have an aim?', in *Authority, Responsibility and Education*, London 1959, pp. 83–95.

6. Wolfgang Brezinkg: *Von der Paedagogik zur Erziehungs-Wissenschaft*, Weinheim/Berlin/Basel, 1971.

7. W. K. Frankena: 'Educational Values and Goals,' in: *Theories of Value and Problems of Education*, ed. by Philip G. Smith, Urbana/Chicago/London 1970, pp. 99–108.

8. Wolfgang Bezinka: *Erziehung als Lebenshilfe*, Wien, 1967, p. 144.

9. *Sophia Perennis*, the Bulletin of the Imperial Iranian Academy of Philosophy, supplement no. 1, Tehran, September 1975, p. 6.

10. Ghazzālī, Kīmīyā-ye-Saʻādat (Alchemy of Happiness) Third edition, Tehran 1345 (1966), p. 11.

11. *Selections from Gandhi*, by Nirmal Kumar Rose, Ahmedabad 1957, Chapter XIX (on Education), p. 283.

12. Frithjof Schuon: *Spiritual Perspectives and Human Facts*, London 1969, p. 17.

13. Sharifi, Hadi: 'Erziehung im Spanungs feld von Tradition und Modernitaet-am Beispiel Persiens', in *Paedagogische Rundschau*, 30. Jg. Heft 11, 1926 S. 8130825.

14. Toshihiko Izutsul 'Two Dimensions of Ego Consciousness in Zen', in: *Sophia Perennis*, vol. II, no. 1, Tehran 1976, pp. 19–37; 'The Mythopeic Ego in Shamanism and Taoism' in *Sophia Perennis*, vol. II, no. 2, Tehran 1976, pp. 22–47.
S. H. Nasr: *Sufi Essays*, London 1972. Frithjof Schuon: *Gnosis*, London 1959. Martin Lings: *What is Sufism*, London 1975.

15. A. K. C. Ottaway: *Education and Society*, London 1962, pp. 10–11.

16. Quran: XLVII, 15.

17. Quran: XXVIII, 88.

18. Quran: VII, 179.

19. S. H. Nasr: *Islamic Science*, London 1976, p.4.
In his other works, the author deals with the question of unity in Islamic thought and culture; see also:
Islam and the Plight of Modern Man, London 1976.
Sacred Art in Persian Culture, Ipswich (England) 1971.

20. Frithjof Schuon: *Understanding Islam*, London and Tonbridge 1963, pp. 22–33.

21. Quran: LXXVI, 1.

22. Quran: LXXXIX, 28.

23. *The Mathnawi of Jalāl al-Dīn Rūmī*, trans. by: R. A. Nicholson, Vol. II, London 1972, p. 5.

24. Quran: LXXVI, 2.

25. Quran: LV, 29.

26. Saʻadi's *Diwan*, Tehran 1317 (1938), p. 217.

27. Quran: LXXVI, 2.

28. Quran: LXXVI, 30.
29. Quran: XXVI, 37–40.
30. Quran: XV, 22.
31. Quran: XXIII, 91.
32. Frithjof Schuon: *Logic and Transcendence*, translated by P. N. Townsend, New York/Evanston/San Francisco/London 1975, p. 12.
33. Quran: XXXVI, 78.
34. Quran: XXXVI, 77.
35. *Sharh-e Gholshan-e Rāz* (commentary on the Secret Rose Garden), by Muhammad Lāhījī, Tehran, 1337 (1958) p. 10.
36. Quran: XV, 99.
37. Quran: LXXXIV, 6.
38. Frithjof Schuon: No activity without Truth, in: *The Sword of Gnosis*, ed. by J. Needleman, Baltimore, Md. Penguin Books Inc., 1974, p. 27.

Traditional Vis-a-Vis Modern Education: Need for a New Perspective

VI. Traditional Islamic Education — Its Aims and Purposes in the Present Day

1. Al-Ibrashi, M.A. *Education in Islam*, p. 11. Studies in Islam series, The Supreme Council for Islamic Affairs, Cairo, Egypt, 1387 (1967).
2. *The Holy Quran*, Sura III, Verse 110.
3. Ibid. The same verse. The meaning is translated as follows: 'You are the best nation ever brought forth to men, enjoining virtue and forbidding vice and believing in Allah.'
4. Mannheim, Karl and Stewart, W. A. C. *An Introduction to the Sociology of Education*, pp. 161–162, Routledge and Kegan Paul, London, 1962.
5. Ibn Khaldoun *The Muqaddima*, pp. 397–398 also Al-Ahwani, M. F. *Education in Islam*, p. 100 also Al-Qabisi *Treatise on Education* edited by Al-Ahwani in the same vol. p. 282.
6. See, for instance, Ibn Sahnoun *Treatise on Child Education* edited by Al-Ahwani the same vol. pp. 353–354.
7. Al-Ahwani ibid. p. 75.
8. Ibid, p. 141 ff. c.f. Ibn Khaldoun *Muqaddima* where he counsels against severity.
9. Ibid. pp. 102–103.
10. The schools of law are unanimous in their prohibition of upholding the letter of the law while breaking its spirit. The Prophet (peace be upon him) cautioned those who might win a court case through eloquence rather than in accordance with the true spirit of the law that they would receive Allah's wrath.
11. This was the system in, among others, Al-Azhar mosque university until its re-organization early this century.
12. Al-Ahwani, op. cit. pp. 253–254. Admittedly the wealthy classes hired private tutors for their children but there were no 'public school systems' or schools for the privileged.
13. Al-Ghazali *Ihya' Ulum Al-Din*, vol. 1, p. 46. Al-Ghazali maintains that no fees should ever be accepted by the teacher. This is a variance with the common practice in his day.

14. Tibbawi, A. L. *Islamic Education*, p. 40, Luzac & Co., London, 1972.
15. Ibn Khaldoun *Muqaddima*, pp. 397–398.
16. Al-Ahwani, op. cit. p. 110.
17. Badawi, M. A. Zaki *The Reformers of Egypt*, Introduction p. 9. The Muslim Institute Papers 2, 1976.
18. Spencer, Herbert *Education*, p. 47, Watts & Co., London, 1945.
19. Hodgson, H. G. S. *Modernity and the Islamic Heritage*, Islamic Studies, vol. 1, p. 115.
20. Friend J. W. and Feibleman, J. *Science and the Spirit of Man*, passim especially pp. 21–63, Allen & Unwin Ltd, London, 1933.
21. Soudan, M. Z. A. *Prayer in Islam*, p. 165, Cairo, 1976.
22. Hadith Sharif.